My Twice-Lived Life

Also by Donald M. Murray

Nonfiction
Writing to Deadline: The Professional Journalist at Work
Creating a Life in Essay, Story, Poem
Writer in the Newsroom
The Craft of Revision
Shoptalk: Learning to Write with Writers
Expecting the Unexpected
Read to Write
Write to Learn
Writing for Your Readers
Learning by Teaching
Write to Communicate: The Language Arts in Process
A Writer Teaches Writing
The World of Sound Recording
Man Against Earth

Fiction
The Man Who Had Everything

MY
TWICE-LIVED
LIFE

A Memoir

DONALD M. MURRAY

BALLANTINE BOOKS • NEW YORK

A Ballantine Book
Published by The Ballantine Publishing Group

Copyright © 2001 by Donald M. Murray

This book contains quotes from:
Plant Dreaming Deep by May Sarton, published
by W. W. Norton and Co., Inc. Copyright © 1968 by May Sarton.
Escaping Into the Open: The Art of Writing True by Elizabeth Berg,
published by HarperCollins. Copyright © 1999 by Elizabeth Berg.
An Autobiography by Anthony Trollope,
published by Doubleday. Copyright © by Anthony Trollope.
Life Work by Donald Hall, published by Beacon Press.
Copyright © 1993 by Donald Hall.

www.randomhouse.com/BB/

Library of Congress Cataloging-in-Publication Data
Murray, Donald Morison, 1924–
My twice-lived life : a memoir of aging / Donald M. Murray.
p. cm.
ISBN 0-345-43690-3
1. Murray, Donald Morison, 1942– 2. Journalists—United
States—Biography. 3. Aging. I. Title.
PN4874.M86 A3 2001
070'.92—dc21

[B]   2001025477

Text design by Ann Gold

Manufactured in the United States of America

First Edition: June 2001

10   9   8   7   6   5   4   3   2   1

CONTENTS

My Twice-Lived Life

Chapter 1

MY UNEXPECTED LIFE

I was in Bayfront Medical Center in St. Petersburg, Florida, far from my New Hampshire home, less than three months after my early retirement at sixty-two, when the nurses—male and female—had given me their cheery bed-and-breakfast welcome to cardiac intensive care and hooked me up to tubes and wires. I experienced an unexpected comfort from the machines and felt my feet and hands, then legs and arms, then body and head relax. I was not anxious as I had been in the restaurant. I no longer felt foolish at asking my friend Chip Scanlan to take me on a careening drive across town to emergency. The nurses had called a doctor, someone from the business office had personally checked my insurance card even if it was Sunday night, and they had taken me seriously enough to admit me to cardiac intensive care. I knew I was where I belonged.

Soon the monitors beeped insistent messages only the nurses could understand, and I was touched by their sudden concern as they circled me, anxiously looking down, each busy with a different task. Then I realized it wasn't caring that motivated them as much as challenge. The smiles became game faces, grim with football-field excitement. They shared an adrenaline high. This would be a "good" heart attack—and as a former police reporter I knew what a "good" fire, accident, shooting meant: one that would test their craft. I imagined I could feel my father's ironic smile on my face and hoped he had known I had made it down to Boston from New Hampshire and was waiting outside emergency while he had had his last heart attack.

Moments later the elephant stepped on my chest— the cliché is accurate—and I knew why the nurses were excited. I was having a heart attack and it must have been a beaut. My first reaction, I confess, was satisfaction. I had been telling my primary-care doctor at home that something was wrong. He assured me he saw no signs of heart trouble.

I was given a stress test by this doctor who called himself a heart specialist but, I later learned, had failed board certification many times, and he told me I didn't need a cardiologist and not to worry. I tried. My father had been a hypochondriac, and I had feared all my life that it was an inherited disease. Fear of his hypochondria was a major reason I played football, boxed, and volunteered for the paratroops. Now the machines proved I was not imagining my failing heart. I gloated. I could hardly wait to tell those doctors when I got home. Then the editor took over: *if* I got home.

I turned my mind from the satisfaction that this was indeed a genuine, 100 percent heart attack to observe just what was going on. I was not surprised at my reporter's detachment. I had a lifetime of training in objective observation. It had served me well when I had to witness the suffering of others and to write their stories on deadline. Now I would see if that coldness that I was both proud and ashamed of could be turned on myself.

A loudspeaker rasped out orders from a cardiologist who had seen me earlier and gone home. The nurses relayed numbers to him and followed orders, inserting needles in me, attaching more wires, feeding medication into tubes, and carrying on a terse dialogue that was similar to the radio messages that went from platoon to company or company to battalion when I was in combat. I appreciated the flat, unemotional manner in which they reported and the equally objective manner of his response. They were businesslike and that was what I wanted at the moment: professional care—very professional care. I focused on their application of technology and listened intently trying to read their medical jargon and find out how I was doing.

My detachment from my own dying did not surprise me. It came from my nature, from experience, from professional training, and from age. We old-timers have been down this route before. We know how to behave or, at least, how we behave in moments of crisis. We have been tested and have usually found ourselves stronger than we expected. One doctor—young, of course—told me that the elderly feel less pain than the young. That may be true, but I like to believe it is more that we are experienced with pain. We know how to confront pain; we know that—so far—the worst waves of pain have passed and life has gone on.

In times of stress, most members of my generation reach back to the myths of our ethnicity. I am a Scot. I am tough; we confront terror with a joke. We'd better have a sense of humor if our men wear skirts to war. While feeling the tremendous pain of a major heart attack, I tried to joke it away—"Haven't you got a smaller elephant?" My audience was too busy to laugh—or perhaps I just wasn't funny.

I could, however, feel myself detaching from myself, an ability I became aware of in the flat we left when I was only four years old. We lived with my mother's mother, a truly tough, commanding, and demanding widow with a great bun of auburn hair and a direct line to our Baptist God. When she called Him the line was never busy. I was aware, even then, that when she made it clear to Mother that she hadn't measured up—letting the tea steep too long, spending too much time shopping with her friends—Mother would meet Father at the door and I would get a beating. Sometimes I hid before he came home, but I never felt it was a personal act; I could detach myself from the whiplash pain of the leather shaving strap. I knew all about cause and effect.

My childhood ability to detach myself from my family and develop an only child loneliness I came to enjoy, served me well in the loneliness of infantry warfare. During the war, I remember realizing one day that I felt happy. I was back from the front, a few hundred yards back, the sun was bright, and I was enjoying lunch, even the dreaded turdlike fruit bar. I was relaxed sitting in a field of corpses, ignoring the dead and even the not-yet dead. All of us who survived infantry combat in the war of our generation would always feel guilty at our ability to detach ourselves from our emotions—fear, terror, panic—and do what had to be done. And beside our guilt stood pride. As the nurses fought to save my life, I felt confident I could take whatever discomfort was necessary to survive.

I wanted to live, but I was wise enough, experienced enough, to know that at this stage the fight would be a passive one. I would give myself over to the nurses and not make their task difficult by flailing away at what I couldn't control. I kept concentrating on my unexpected calm, remembering when I first got over my fear of water and learned to float. I imagined I was again lying just under the surface of Lake Millen at Camp

Morgan, my face above water. I saw again the bowl of sky, the pines that ran down to the lake's edge, felt the easy rise and fall of lake water.

As the nurses worked harder and the foot of the elephant did not rise from my chest, a long, brightly lit tube rose up from intensive care and at the other end stood Lee, the daughter who had died ten years before, standing in the favorite blue jumper she had made herself, smiling, her hand raised in a hesitant wave.

As I was starting toward her, a male nurse slapped my shoulder as if I had just scored a touchdown. "It's over. You're going to make it."

"Thanks," I said as Lee, still smiling, waved and disappeared—for now.

In January 1946 I was in the front rows of the 82nd Airborne marching down Fifth Avenue in New York City in the World War II Victory Parade. Then, in 1987, forty-two years after that parade, I could not march the nine-tenths of a mile from home to my office at the University of New Hampshire without resting. My legs felt heavy. I had unexpected moments of apprehension. I put myself in a cardiac exercise program and had trouble circling the gym.

Why didn't I go to a doctor? I did. I kept asking about my symptoms. The doctor didn't worry: I had low cholesterol. I knew that. I was approaching the anniversary of my father's first heart attack—and he had low cholesterol. The doctor smiled and nodded but made no notes. Only now, in allowing myself to tell this story, can I admit the frustration, the anger, and the uncomfortable, even stupid, fatalism that I let guide my life.

I had passed the stress test I had requested, but I had trouble walking the slight incline from downtown to Ham Smith Hall, not much more than a quarter of a mile. I was only sixty-two and my appearance contributed to my undoing. I was almost six feet three inches tall and walked the vigorous, manly walk I had practiced in front of the mirror so I would get beaten up less—I hoped—on the way to school or home. I didn't look sickly. But something was going on. I retired from the university in September, and that month my daughter Hannah tells me I told her that if I died, to go ahead with her October wedding to Michael as scheduled. I know she is telling the truth, but I still do not remember saying that, but I do remember the suppressed—well, almost suppressed—apprehension of those months after retirement.

A former student had recommended a specialist in Boston who put me on a regimen of fish oil and niacin and I don't remember what else. He took credit for the low cholesterol I had inherited. The symptoms persisted. I asked my family doctor to recommend another cardiologist. He told me I didn't need one, that he could take care of me just fine. What I didn't know until I asked for and received my medical records after my heart attack is that I had suffered the prejudice suffered by most women. I was a writer. It was my imagination. Writers are emotional.

Still, I went to make an appointment with the cardiologist. His appointment clerk told me I couldn't see him for six weeks. I accepted her statement. I would not do so today. Before my heart attack, I was an agreeable, affable patient: I did not want to offend the doctor who might save my life. Now I am an aggressive patient. If I think I need attention, I demand it. I was in Florida on a business trip two days before my appointment with the cardiologist when the elephant stomped on my chest.

Monday morning after my heart attack I was given an angiogram. For some reason I admitted I was a veteran, and it turned out the male nurse and the female technicians had all been in the military. We spoke the black humor of combat, and I had to live the myth of the tough paratrooper. Indeed, I felt no fear in watching the pictures on the screen. The diagnosis was clear to me. The area around my heart looked like the Mississippi delta country I had flown over. Barges clogged the river; channels must be cleared. I felt a strange confidence that I—not so much the surgeons but I— could do what had to be done. And beneath the military kidding between staff and patient was a surprising tenderness. I was beginning to understand what

I had read about: the importance of touch in medical care. The male nurse who held a pad tightly against the artery in the groin through which the camera had snaked not only staunched the bleeding but communicated a calm competence. I was literally in good hands.

Later that day the doctor told me I needed a triple bypass, then read me a long list of what could go wrong and made me watch a VCR tape of what would happen and, again, what could go wrong. Still I felt a wonderful, irrational confidence. I had suffered the long-feared heart attack. I was tough; I could take it. The adrenaline kicked in. I heard a group of doctors in the hall discussing a case. Then I realized I was the case when one of them began a sentence, "If we can keep him alive until Wednesday . . ."

I called out, "Care to come in and explain that?"

They were horrified, thinking I could not hear them as they consulted, but they explained that they wanted the first team and Wednesday was the best day for that, but if anything started to go wrong, they could assemble a surgical team on Tuesday.

Even then I felt no special apprehension. I would do what needed to be done, and I realized I had recovered my writer's distance, a quality of standing back and observing myself and others that I had often thought was a curse, a cold reporter's detachment.

Now I blessed the distance and was able to dictate a *Boston Globe* column to my wife, Minnie Mae, that

Tuesday, not out of a compulsive, workaholic person- ality but out of a need for naming. Writers know that if you name the terrors, they retreat. Note the specific details, the glint of light from the surgeon's knife, the intense glare from the light above, the chill of the open- heart surgical room, and the terrors become less intimi- dating in some way I do not fully understand.

I thought the operation went well when I woke to see my family smiling down at me, but later I learned that they had gone to Chip Scanlan's home, eaten chili in celebration, and then were suddenly called back to the hospital. I was bleeding to death. A nurse spotted the problem, prepped me, and rushed me back into surgery while my family and Chip waited for hours.

I was told I would lose a day in my life and that I should be glad I did. My family assures me that it was a good day to lose. I felt discomfort but no pain when I became conscious. I remember Hannah hooking me up to my Walkman and playing Mozart's fifteenth and six- teenth piano concertos that had been thoughtfully taped by Tom French, then a young reporter on the *St. Peters- burg Times*. I remember the bed being cranked up so I could eat—a greasy non-cardiac-diet hamburger of all things—and the enormous effort it took to spear a small bite and then slowly, ever so slowly raise it to my mouth and chew—slowly.

My slow eating was impatiently observed by my daughters and Minnie Mae until suddenly she could stand it no more and swooped down and scooped the whole piece of pumpkin pie and gulped it down while her daughters belly-laughed and I croaked something that sounded like laughter. I was alive. I could laugh. We could laugh together.

I made goals. I would walk as long if not as fast as the tiny ninety-four-year-old Jewish lady who had her bypass at the same time I had mine. I received phone calls and messages from friends all over the country. As an odd, only child, I had always hoped for the love of friends; now their affection almost overwhelmed me.

The hospital was not a restful place. It never is. As I fell asleep one night, I was wakened to be weighed in an elephant sling. They weighed me in grams! Another night I woke with a start. A male nurse who had helped save my life was standing by the bed. I was indebted to him, but he was, well, a nerd. A very serious young man whom I would never have asked for sexual advice, yet here he was telling me that despite my normal anxieties I would be able to have erections and complete sex acts in the surprisingly near future. I could hardly keep from giggling. My anxieties at the time were about breathing. I didn't listen for the drumbeat of passion, just the routine old regular beat of a working heart.

My huge black roommate, a bulldozer operator, couldn't keep from laughing, too. After the nurse left we howled. I can't remember my roommate's name, but I remember his humor, wisdom, concern. We talked day and night, and he introduced me to the board of deacons from his church when they came to call, and they paid me the great compliment of allowing me to share in the humor and the music of their conversation, which rose and fell in the call-and-response tradition that was like music to my white ears. We did write after I left, but too soon I had a letter from his widow saying how much our friendship meant to him. It certainly meant a great deal to me.

My next roommate was also an African American, a former principal of a segregated high school, who was surprised by my first question, "How much has been lost by integration?" He told me that a culture had been lost. He did not glorify the days of the 1970s when black teachers had to raise their own money for the tenth month of salary while white teachers were paid out of city funds. His school never had a new textbook, but they did have a common culture that was lost when the pot melted white.

I reveled in the companionship of my roommates, in the nurses, in my wife, daughters, and the new son-in-law, who told a client that he had to be with me. I could feel myself get stronger by the minute. Others on the floor loudly and constantly complained that they were irregular. I couldn't care less. I was alive. I had another unexpected life to live.

Then, five days after the operation, as we drove to the rented condo where my family had been staying to begin this life, we stopped at a huge drug store at St. Petersburg Beach. I wandered away and found myself alone in a long aisle. I was no longer wired to the nurse's station. I no longer could push a button and receive immediate help. I could not see my wife or daughter. I was alone.

The panic began. The tightening band around my chest, the almost vertigo, the trouble breathing, the awareness of my pounding heart, louder than I had ever heard it. I realized in that moment that I would often feel the symptoms of fear that are the same as the symptoms of another heart attack. I had survived the week-long, immediate testing of a heart attack and surgery, but now I would have to learn a different skill of alert patience, read my body, know that there would be many false alarms, but almost inevitably some day— or night—the elephant would again place his foot on my chest and lean down.

Chapter 2

A MATTER OF IDENTITY

Months later I was back home in New Hampshire with my unexpected life stretching out before me. I had my father's heart attack and survived, and I had the retirement plan he never had. I had the physical and economic freedom to begin a new life. I remember a lightness, a freedom to do what I wanted to in my own way, but I knew that freedom often brings fear. We see this with nations and we see it with individuals who talk retirement but keep pushing the date back.

When I was chairperson of the English department at the University of New Hampshire we had that wonderful gift that a few wise corporations have adopted—the sabbatical. Professors could, in their seventh year, have a semester off with full pay or a year off with half pay, but then I found that a few of my colleagues would cancel their leaves at the last moment, and one faculty member had never taken a sabbatical. We all know people who talk and plan early retirement, but when the opportunity arrives they remain at work. Work—even hated work—is their identity. Years ago I had covered the closing of a New Hampshire textile mill and I returned, days later, to interview former workers, young and old, women and men, who came each morning, lunch box in hand, to stand by the gate that would never open. I can still hear the rushing water that had made this an ideal mill site two hundred years earlier; I can still see the black staring windows of the closed mill. And I can hear the terrible weight of the silence rising from looms that would never again clatter through day shift and night shift. It was such mills that brought my family to this country, and I could understand the workers who, generation after generation, had gone to work in the mill.

I can also remember my own fear of retiring early even when I had writing I wanted to do. I was sixty-one and grumping about all my conflicting jumble of obligations, responsibilities, and deferred dreams when my good and wise friend Don Graves told me to list all the activities I was doing, *in the order of the time I was spending on them*. I knew I was a busy college professor, preparing my classes, reading students' papers and meeting with each student every week in an individual conference, researching, writing, giving talks and running workshops, consulting, and scurrying along the gerbil treadmill of campus politics. When I made the list, I found I had thirteen different strands in my professional life, and for all my bellyaching, I wanted to do all of them. I had long ago earned the seniority and power to control much of my professional life and learned to say no to the tasks that did not interest me. But then Don told me to number the thirteen activities I was doing, in red, *according to my own desires*. Number one for what I wanted to do most, number two next, and so on. The list was precisely reversed. Even numbers seven and eight were in inverse order. What I wanted to do most I was doing least; what I wanted to do least I was doing most.

Still I didn't act. Once we master our jobs we feel a sense of comfort if not accomplishment. Our jobs, even ones we proclaim that we hate, are our identity in this society. We are the plumber, the insurance agent, the lawyer, the contractor, the druggist, the police officer, the professor, the sales representative, the accountant, the manager, the senior employee, the coffee-machine historian. We have a place. My generation, the children of the Depression, had an understandable addiction to expectedness. We had tasted insecurity in the Depression and the war and could not quite trust security. We chose to work for the phone company, the bank, the corporation that, we thought then, made a career-long commitment to its workers. We might swagger as if we were dashing combat veterans willing to take risks, but in fact we were chained to the expected paycheck, the expected parking place, the expected corner office, the expected vacation, the expected power and status, forever comforted by the known.

My body had told me earlier that it was time to retire from teaching at the university, but I wasn't listening. To become a man I learned to practice the manly art of denial. I played with pain on the football field and took a graduate course in denial as a paratrooper.

I lived less than a mile from my office, but I had to sit on a flat-topped piece of granite and rest halfway there. One day as I sat on that stone, I took Don's list out of my shirt pocket and wondered if I could afford to retire.

My father never had a retirement plan. He had all sorts of success plans, but they never worked out for long. He had debts and to pay them off fell for schemes such as the Morris Plan that consolidated the debts into a bigger debt. His father had been head maintenance man at Filene's, and when he died young, his oldest son—my father—was hired by Mr. Filene himself.

Father began as a stock clerk, worked up to be a floor walker, one of those elegantly dressed men who patrolled the best department stores to help the lady shoppers and to watch for shoplifters. Father became a buyer of ladies' silk stockings and gloves and dreamt of the store he did open on West Street in Boston in 1932 at the bottom of the Depression and lost a few years later. He worked for most of the big department stores in Boston, rising from buyer to merchandise manager, then losing his job and getting another, which he would lose. At the momentary height of his success, he was elected deacon in the mercantile Christianity of the downtown Tremont Temple Baptist Church, where 2,700 worshippers filled the two balconies on Sunday evenings. He wore a morning coat, vest, and striped trousers and sat on the platform during services.

He entertained at the Parker House dining room next door to Tremont Temple, where dignified waiters, called colored gentlemen by my family, wore white gloves as they served us. Even as a child I was embarrassed by their dignified manners that implied we were better than they were. I suspect they knew behind their smiling masks, as so many others did, that we lived a life of dignified fraud on loans and gifts and charges against friends' department store accounts.

When Father's pay would be garnisheed I would have to go to whatever department store kept him on the payroll and say he was sick and beg an illegal advance. To my shame, they knew—and knew I knew they knew—and gave me some folded bills. I hated their kindness and swore my children would never have to do this—and they haven't.

When I was a boy we never paid anything on time or in full. Relatives who made far less than my father in the Great Depression hired Mother to type or paid her to take care of my paralyzed grandmother. We lived on their charity and paid the price of a bitter generosity given with scorn.

I knew nothing about handling the money I had saved and the funds that would come to me in retirement, so I applied to a financial planner and was surprised to be accepted as a client. I filled out pages of questions about my fiscal condition, a term that I thought belonged to someone on the other side of the tracks. When we met in the planner's dark-paneled conference room, I remember the physical shock when I realized the financial adviser was saying I could easily afford to retire early.

I had been pushing against a locked door all my life, and it suddenly flew open. I stumbled into a condition of financial security I could not imagine I would really achieve even when saving toward it. I was surprised, delighted, disoriented, and half-unbelieving. I have heard many other men and women who grew up in the Depression express their own astonishment at such news. We had worked to survive and found we had prospered.

My wife, who handled our accounts, had been brought up in Kentucky on the fragile edge of poverty. As I write this, the stock market is once more in one of its tumbles and most people are surprised. Not those of our generation. The prosperity of the 1970s, '80s, and '90s seemed unnatural. We came from a different world. It is difficult for my children to comprehend the economic world before World War II when I knew only a few people fortunate enough to pay a mortgage and not rent; impossible for my grandchildren to imagine a world when shoes were resoled or fitted with metal taps, pens worn down to the nub, and penny candy too expensive to buy.

On the drive home from that paneled conference room I became again the small boy at the bottom of the stairway that led from the second-floor flat to the side door, facing the landlord who wore a great felt hat that shaded his face, his shoulders huge inside his overcoat, his hand held out waiting for the rent. I told him again the story about my father's sickness that my mother, hidden but listening at the top of the stairs, had taught me. We couldn't pay this month. We'll pay some. Soon. Dad was sick abed. Grandma was still paralyzed and Mother's leg was worse.

He knew about Mother's leg and all the rest. He looked down on me and his hard landlord's face broke into a gentle smile, and that made it worse. I'd rather have shame than pity. He knew us all too well. He knew the deacon's wife was at the top of the stairs coaching the deacon's son in lying. And like the bookkeepers at the store, he knew that I knew he knew. I had his unwelcome pity—and a month's rent delayed. He would not dispossess us as he had the couple downstairs.

I had watched through the lace curtains of my

sleeping-porch bedroom when the couple downstairs faced court officials with badges who arrived and ordered moving men to pile their furniture in heaps across the sidewalk. Each spring and fall junk pickup, I see the piles of discarded stuff pop up along our streets and remember that furniture on the sidewalk and taste the old bitter fear that this might happen to us.

I will always be the boy hired at Miller's Market, the butcher apron, man-sized, triple-folded around my waist, seeing my mother's name on the bad-debt, give-no-credit list by the wall phone where housewives called in their delivery orders. When I went to get my first fifty-cent pay for a twelve-hour day, I found my mother had charged against it, and I had to persuade Mr. Miller not to let my mother do that.

In the first grade I had already resolved not to be beholden, not to live a life of shame, of lies, of apology, of asking for an extension. I would, in the terms of my childhood, become "a good provider." And now, I had done it. I owned a single-family home of my middle-class dreams and a car in the garage, as well. I had no debts and no loans, some money in the bank, and a retirement plan that would pay me what I had put in and then some.

But still, I found, there was that matter of identity. Home in New Hampshire after the bypass, parka hood up, mittens on, retired, I walked my half mile, then my mile, then my two miles, paying equal respect to the bright December sun or the dark gray winter clouds that press down against the roadside pines, celebrating cold as well as warmth, even taking delight in the small pain of ice rain pricking my cheeks—I hurt, therefore I am—a survivor newly aware of the muscles that press each foot against the earth and propel him forward.

Having long ago left the born-again religion of my parents, I am amused that I feel born again into a life of my own making. I am retired. I have eating money and walking-around money. I have a partner who has always supported my dreams. My children are all on their own. I can be anything I want.

Well, almost. I have been to the Arctic in Alaska and Norway, but I will never be an Arctic explorer following a team of dogs across the desolate ice I find so fascinating. I will never play defensive end for the New England Patriots, charging in to sack the passer. I will not even do the things I *could* do: buy a Harley, learn to fly, travel around the world on tramp steamers. My real dreams are more modest: travel, read, collect classical CDs, draw, and, most of all, have quiet moments in which I am surprised by what appears on my page.

I will not even move from the small college town of Durham, New Hampshire, in which we live to an island off the coast of Maine or Nova Scotia, build a mountain home in Vermont, own an apartment smack-dab in the middle of Manhattan, lease a house perched on a fiord in Norway or on an island in the Hebrides. I wanted to move when I retired, but Minnie Mae declared wisely that we should wait a year. She was right. We have remained in the house we built when we came to Durham in 1963.

Now I have another life to design. Some people are blessed with an acceptance of themselves that astounds me; they are what they are, the world be damned. Minnie Mae is Minnie Mae. She behaves the same for everyone. A friend, John Gaumond, said the other day, "I have always been John." He knows who he is and accepts it, always has. I have been the twentieth-century American moving across the frontiers of class, social status, geography, ethnicity, and religion, trying on masks and costumes, finding that I do fool most of the people most of the time, but not myself. I feel a fraud and now, in this unexpected life, have the opportunity to continue to work my way back to who I am.

When I was young there was a great deal of talk about the self-made man. My father, who was never quite able to make himself, greatly admired such men. They were entrepreneurs, men—never women—of lowly beginnings who became rich by vim and vigor combined with a shrewd eye. Shrewd was considered good. There were a number of such men on the board of deacons who sat on the platform behind the pulpit at Tremont Temple Baptist Church wearing expressions of pious self-satisfaction.

Now that I approach the age when my father passed

away, I realize that his business failures ironically made him a truly religious man. In the decades of debts and humiliation, he developed an increasing compassion for the lonely, the aged, the forgotten, and he remade himself into a pastor without ordination, running a religious program for the elderly. When he died I found several hundred names of people, most who had no family, many others whose family denied them, who had given my father's name as the one who should bury them and dispose properly of what property they had.

Looking back from the perspective of my bypass, I realize how I have been self-made, how often we are all self-made. This doesn't mean I am unaware of genetics, economic trends, sociological influences, the forces of history, and plain old-fashioned luck, but it seems that we make decisions that change the course of our lives.

We are often given a role to play, struggle to fit it, and then, if we are lucky, escape into another role. Each year of school, from first grade until sixth, I played the role of victim or Christian martyr, if you want to dramatize it. I was the bully's delight, first a chubby butterball, then suddenly a string bean, but always an entertainment for my classmates, usually led by a far smaller, far tougher kid named, I believe, Tommy McDonald. He would swagger up before school, after school, or at recess and give me a punch, then another, and another. He particularly liked to get me backed up to the huge pipe flagpole so my head caused the metal to ring as the back of my skull connected with it. I never retaliated. Mother had told me that if I truly believed in Jesus Christ, the bully's hand would be stayed. I didn't believe hard enough; the bully's knuckles connected.

I came home bloodied and bowed, and Mother would herd me into the small, dark brown room to the right of the front door on Vassell Street, make me kneel and place my head on her knee where I almost swooned at her woman's smell, and commanded me to pray for a stronger faith. Then she ordered me back to school—taking my hand and dragging me along in the beginning—for another Christian testing. And yet another failure of faith.

I never blamed Tommy or the other boys. I never blamed my mother. I never blamed Jesus. I blamed myself. I had insufficient faith. I kept trying to believe so hard it hurt, scowling my face into belief, tightening all my muscles as if that could bring belief. And then one day in the sixth grade, after six years of religious failure, Walter Almada brushed by me as we were standing in line after recess.

Walter Almada had never bullied me. His father, Mel Almada, was right fielder for the Boston Red Sox. He was, I believe, the first Mexican player for the Sox. Historical note: Red Sox players in the 1930s lived in rented flats in working-class neighborhoods. They stood far lower on the economic scale than tool-and-die makers.

Some instinct told me I couldn't battle my way through all the bullies in the sixth grade but if I could beat the crap out of the best athlete in the class, I'd have a new life. I did. It took several teachers to tug me off Walter Almada as I kept banging his head against a granite curb. The amazing thing was that he understood what I had to do. We didn't become friends, I never could have belonged to the athletic elite of the Massachusetts Field School, but he treated me with a dignified respect—and the rest of the boys stayed clear.

Then, in still another life, when I played the role of soldier, I was in Piccadilly Circus in London in 1944, on leave, wearing a Class A paratroop uniform, jump wings, and polished boots, when a seaman with submariner insignia swaggered by me, stopped, took a look at me, then a second look, and a third as I broke out laughing. It was Tommy McDonald, who used to make the flagpole ring with my skull not so very many years earlier.

The women's movement made me realize how much I had been shaped by a male world in which conflict was glorified and helped me admit to myself, then others, how much I hated conflict. I boxed, I argued, I played football, I shot at the enemy, I asked hostile questions as a reporter, I dueled my way through courtyards and back alleys of campus politics, I learned to puff up and confront, threaten, and, yes, probably bully—we often become those we fear—but I did not like conflict in any form. And the better I was at conflict, the more I was aware that this was not me, not the me with whom I could be comfortable.

But it seems that to get ahead we have to wear costumes we once scorned. After the war I made myself into an A student in college, the high school flunk-out becoming cum laude; then the former military policeman made himself into a police reporter, although I often became nauseous before—or even during—an interview but still asked the questions they did not want asked. I made myself into a husband twice, a father three times, a magazine writer, a freelancer, a college professor, each time uncomfortable in the role I played but also proud I could carry it off.

I had done what the world expected of me. I had practiced and achieved the manly handshake and the direct look in the eye my father so valued. Few of us seem comfortable in the person we have made ourselves to satisfy our families, friends, teachers, employers, but it is necessary for us to graduate from school, fight a war, hold a job, raise a family, collect a salary, vest our health and retirement plans. We dance to the tune required.

In retirement, I feared I would become a feeble, hesitant old man. I had seen my father shrink and his collars become large, his confidence seeping slowly away. I feared I would become the apologetic old man without confidence.

Perhaps it was, at sixty-three, time to grow up, to give up the dreams of what isn't yet written, to put aside the drives and ambitions and just be, well, an old man. My father's hypochondria became justified after his heart attack, but despite that, he went into church work when he retired from business.

I looked about me for other retirement models and saw a former dean sitting on his lawn pulling up tiny weeds. Not me. Another retiree putters. He has the best organized garage in the western world. Now he is reorganizing it. Nope. Not for me. Others golf or fish. Save me from those fates.

I see the old men sitting in rings around the planters and fountains at the mall. Waiting. Waiting. I try sitting beside them. There is no comradeship here. Silence. Loneliness.

I went back home, opened my daybook, and started to write following the ancient Roman advice I had followed for so many years—*nulla dies sine linea*, not a day without a line. I wrote a word that led to more words. I forgot I was old, that I had suffered a heart attack. I became what I was and had been, a writer, still an apprentice to the craft that I would, thankfully, never learn.

Chapter 3

LIVING BACKWARDS

And so I began the journey of aging, a rafting trip down a river I thought familiar but that became more unfamiliar—and faster—the further I traveled. I thought I had known the river of aging better than most. All my years before I left for college and for war we lived with my grandmother. She really raised me and was my closest playmate during many of my early years. Later, after her "shock," which was what we called a stroke, she lay paralyzed. I became her nurse.

In another life, when my widowed mother-in-law lost the sister with whom she lived, I was the one, not my wife, who invited her to live with us. It was a virtuous mistake, wrong for her and wrong for us; she turned into an old lady in the nine years—of the first twelve years of our marriage—when she lived with us. Again I observed aging firsthand.

But as Minnie Mae and I aged, I realized I had always been an outsider, similar to a military historian who had never been to war. I knew a lot about aging as a caretaker, as one who is empathetic to the problems of aging, who always liked the company of old people but had always *imagined* what the elderly must feel and think, never riding the raft myself, never negotiating the roiling rapids of aging, the swift currents, the unexpected pools of drifting quiet, never experiencing these terrors and pleasures firsthand.

I had sped through life, proudly thinking I was outracing those around me, taking summer school courses to do three years of college in two, looking ahead to the next job, planning the future while rocketing through the present. Sometimes I felt guilty about this, usually when someone said I should feel guilty. They said I should slow down, savor the moment, but there were bills to pay, obligations to fulfill, opportunities to seize, ambition to satisfy—while discovering that feeding ambition only increases the hunger.

Aging would bring the answer. Ambition would be satisfied; few new opportunities would be offered; obligations would be cast off; the bills would be paid by a pension, by savings turned into investments, and by Social Security. I would live comfortably at a slower pace, savoring each hour as I sat in my morris chair, feet up on a hassock, contemplating my woods and the life I had lived.

But life accelerates with age. Your step may slow, your memory search mechanism may become creaky, but life moves faster than ever before. Turn off this week's *Antiques Roadshow* and next week's comes on.

I was, of course, aware of many of the disadvantages of old age, but few of the advantages. The disadvantages were not what I imagined and the advantages far more than I ever thought. These have been the best years of my life, and the terrors—which have made the pleasures even greater—have often not been what I expected.

I felt surprisingly well prepared for the trip. I did not fear or fight age as so many of my contemporaries did. I was looking forward to being an old man, young for his age, of course, even—admit it—a bit smug about how well I would age. I had not suffered the fear of age so many suffer in a youth culture. I rather liked my gray hair and beard turning white. I felt I had earned my wrinkles, and wore the brown spots that began to speckle my skin as survivor medals. I never felt myself attractive when young, but now I rather liked the face worn by aging. I thought it showed character.

I saw aging as another adventure and, armed with the reporter's ability to focus on the revealing detail, was prepared to live the experience twice—in the moment and, as is the writer's habit, in the greater reality of reflection afterwards.

I would record the adventure of my own aging, being positive to the end, looking ahead to the next rapids, the slow turning curve, the unexpected view of sky, the phosphorescence in the night river. But I often found my-self living backwards, not forward as I expected, turning in my seat to study where I had been more than where I was going. I asked myself if this was a way of avoiding the obvious destination of this river of age, but I didn't think it was. I was still eager to see what lay ahead, but I was increasingly fascinated by what lay behind.

I had been too busy getting ahead to look back. Most survivors of the Great Depression and World War II were the first in their families to go to college, thanks to the G.I. Bill. We did not live a life of reflection but a life of promotion, focused on the next step on the ladder—and the next, and the next, and the next. We were survivors and continued to live the survivor's life long after it was necessary.

But now, retired, many of us realize we have reached the end of our career ladders, and if we haven't achieved our dreams, we have done better than we expected. In many cases our disappointment in not having climbed higher becomes acceptance, even relief from the pres-sure to achieve, followed by a sense of wonder that we did so well. I have published novels but not written The Novel. I have published poems but not written The Poem. I have, however, published hundreds of articles, more than six hundred columns, more than twenty books, and by writing textbooks on the teaching of writ-ing, won my revenge on the teachers who inspired me to drop out of high school twice before flunking out. I have lived a life of writing that was a far better life than I could have imagined.

Had it been all luck, an ever booming economy, the result of careful planning, the inevitable product of decisions that had implications I could never have known when I made them. Was it genetics, my working alone at my desk the product of some centuries-dead ancestral Scot who fished alone off the Hebrides or hunted alone in the great forest before the Clearances? I liked where I had gotten, but I wasn't sure I knew how I had gotten there, and had an unexpected hunger to know.

I thought I was not one who looked back. I rarely pulled off the highway to look at a house in which we had once lived. I was not much for nostalgia and avoided school, class, and military reunions. But I began to see mistily what might be patterns, connections I had never made at the time, even inevitabilities. I also discovered ironies.

I fled my father, who copied, framed, and sent out Bible verses, to collect, frame, and send out quotations from writers I admire. This morning, for example, I scanned into my computer a quotation from Elizabeth Berg, a fine novelist, that was helping me in the writing of this book, and e-mailed and faxed it to fellow writers. Here's what she said:

I believe that fiction feeds on itself, grows like a pregnancy. The more you write, the more there is to draw from; the more you say, the more there *is* to say. The deeper you go into your imagination, the richer that reservoir becomes. You do not run out of material by using all that's in you; rather, when you take everything that is available one day, it only makes room for new things to appear the next. . . . You don't need to know a whole book in order to write the first page. You don't even need to know the end of the first page. You need only the desire to create something that will say what you feel needs to be said, however vague its form at the beginning. You need a willingness to discover the wealth and wisdom of your own subconscious, and to trust that it will tell you what to do and how to do it— not all at once, but as needed, step by step. You have to take a deep breath, let go of your usual control, and then begin walking in the dark.

I frame it for my desk as my father would frame a statement from a preacher and then I frame another to send to my friend and writing colleague Chip Scanlan. I can hear my father laughing from his Baptist heaven: "Gotcha."

I move back across the years as if I were playing a movie in my head, catching glimpses of the familiar stranger, myself. I am called up to the publisher's office at the old *Boston Herald* at ten o'clock in the morning. All the top editors are standing around grinning, but I don't get it. We are handed champagne glasses, and

mine is poured full just before Bob Choate announces
we have won a Pulitzer for the editorials I have written.
My hand starts to shake and I spill most of the champagne on the floor. I am twenty-nine years old and have
been told I was the youngest winner at the time.

That was one of life's memorable moments, but the
celebration soon ended and I had my three daily editorials to write, but now the crossbar had been raised.
They would be written by a Pulitzer Prize winner.

In my first marriage, we wanted no children, but my
second wife, Minnie Mae, did, so I agreed, full of anxiety about the role of father. I have a snapshot of my father, who lived at home but was a stranger leaving early
returning late all my childhood. In the photo he is holding me as an infant. It may have been the only time he
ever held me. He looks as if someone had handed him
a greased piglet. Then I see the nurse at Beth Israel
hand me the baby that I had been told would probably
be blind. My daughter's eyes meet mine. My arms hold
Anne just fine. I am a father.

The film of memory shows me a paratrooper on my
first night jump, tumbling from the plane into a night
of stars. I am surrounded by stars that seem so close I
could touch each one.

But the film is edited. There are times when I watch
myself in combat and the screen goes blank. I try to run
it forward, backwards, but nothing. There are more
blanks when the camera travels back to my childhood,

but then unexpected images appear. Not all memories are comfortable, but in age what we have tried to forget often floods back. When I am out with Uncle Don for whom I am named, I see this large man, a YMCA director, owner of summer caddie camps, a great shock of white hair and a belly hard as a steel barrel, suggesting as he often did that we pee out of doors. I catch a look at his thing as I did each time we stood together watering a bush. Years later I rerun in memory the eight-millimeter movies he took of boys at his camp running naked to shower and out, twisting, turning, trying to shield themselves from Uncle Don's whirring camera.

I felt it necessary to look back and understand what I could not as a child, to confront the dark mysteries of my childhood. I knew when I grew angry with Minnie Mae that if I stopped and remembered, I was angry at my mother. I knew that I needed affection and I also knew that I felt that was a weakness. Mother had always ridiculed my father's weakness, his need to be liked. I had run from my childhood but not escaped.

Years into my retirement a young woman, the victim of incest and friend of one of my daughters, came to see me for advice about writing her story. As she tells me some of the difficult details, I find myself telling her—to make her less embarrassed—how my mother would take a bar of Ivory soap, cut it away with a kitchen knife while I had to wait knowing what was coming. She cut it down to the shape of a small baseball bat with eight sharp, beveled edges. Then she would bend me over the bathtub edge and with one, swift, hard, unrelenting shove force it up my rectum. She told me, with grim satisfaction, that it would cure—or prevent—constipation.

When I finished the story, my visitor said, "That's sexual abuse." I was staggered by the phrase, and she soon left. I had to go to a meeting in Portsmouth, and as I drove I reran the movie of the frequent scene in the bathroom. When I had confessed the story to Minnie Mae in the first years of our marriage, I had seen myself as a small boy, and in fact, I cannot remember when I did not have a homemade suppository shoved up my rear. I thought every boy and girl received this anticonstipation treatment.

But this night, as I drove to my meeting with the phrase *sexual abuse* that she spat out, angry at my mother, seeing me as a fellow victim, I reluctantly ran the movie again and seeing the hall outside the bathroom through the open door, Grandmother paralyzed in her bed nearby, my father talking church business on the bedroom phone, I realize this is a flat to which we moved when I was fourteen, the place where I grew taller than Mother and Father; tall enough to tell my father that if he hit me again, I would coldcock him; big enough to get night newspaper jobs by saying I was twenty-one, then twenty-two; strong enough to get a football scholarship to a junior college after not graduating from high school; fearless enough to explore—alone—the streets and alleys of Boston; and still my mother bent me over the tub edge and rammed those suppositories up my rear end.

I didn't know how to deal with that, but I knew now I would have to. At the time I went underground. Recently a classmate, Norman Peskin, sent me from his home in the Philippines a picture of our eighth-grade class, and I see myself with a big smile. I recognize the mask I have worn so long it is natural. And it is. I am a friendly old dog, a burly kind of guy, open, the kind of guy who talks with strangers, gives a little of his story, gets a lot of theirs. I know that people like me, but I always feel a fraud. I know the man who lives behind the mask.

As life raced forward I would have to live backwards, the good and the bad, to remember what I had tried so hard to forget and to celebrate so much that was good but had been passed by in the rush of life or passed over as ordinary when it was not.

I have always enjoyed the light at the end of day when the shadows are long and the texture of grass, ledge, water, wall are revealed. Now, rushing forward but living backwards in the evening of my life, I appreciate the texture of my life, the wonder of the ordinary as never before.

Chapter 4

TURNING POINTS

Young people often ask me if I had my life to live over, would I do anything different. I ponder the question I never ask myself and each time say no, but go on to explain this isn't arrogance. I have done stupid things (almost nothing but stupid things from grades one through twelve), made unwise choices, disappointed others and myself, but if I had to do it over again, I would probably make the same decisions.

Today I would not marry my first wife and I'm sure she would not marry me, but in wartime, trying to escape our families, following the social landscape of those years—no living together before marriage as both our daughters did—I think we would have made the same wrong decision. I lived the life I was given with the limited vision of the moment, not with the wisdom of age.

I am struck, however, by those small, often offhand, casual moments on which my life did turn. I'm not talking about the historic events that would change my life. The moment I heard a radio report of the Japanese attack on Pearl Harbor I knew for certain my life would change and it did. Neither am I thinking of those personal moments of obvious transition. When Minnie Mae Emmerich showed up as a substitute blind date it may not have been love at first sight but it certainly was pursuit at first sight and marriage in eleven months. I knew my life would be changed. The moments I'm speaking of have seemed like ordinary events. As time passed I recognized their significance. I found myself thinking back—again and again—to these fleeting moments for wisdom or strength.

One such moment occurred when I was fourteen years old. Mother sent me to Dr. Bartlett for a routine checkup. I rode my bike the two miles to Dr. Bartlett's yellow house on Beale Street in Wollaston, leaned my bike against a tree, locking it carefully in those days when so many like to believe that locks were not necessary. They were. I went up the small porch to his tiny waiting room. No nurse, no appointment, just his regular visiting hours and a crowded circle of patients perched on an odd assortment of kitchen chairs, silently waiting their turn.

Dr. Bartlett was the only authority, other than God, that Grandma and therefore Mother listened to. He made house calls, frequently clumping up the stairs with his black bag full of homeopathic remedies. Grandma lay bedridden from a stroke, Mother had an infected leg with running sores all the years I can remember her, Father took to bed when business dreams confronted reality, and I had a sickly childhood. Dr. Bartlett was the only person who was not family who knew the secrets of our home.

When it was my turn to enter the doctor's office this day and have his cold stethoscope put against my chest, he casually asked, "How are your folks?"

"The usual," I answered, and then apologized, realizing those two words sounded fresh—somehow a betrayal.

Dr. Bartlett, a tall down east Mainer with more than a little American Indian in him, was a tall, commanding man with a hooked nose and small black eyes. He had the exotic smell of tobacco blended with ether when he had come from the operating room. Dr. Bartlett stopped all motion, focused those jet-black eyes on mine, and said slowly and carefully, making each word a sentence, "Donald. You. Do. Not. Have. To. Be. Like. Your. Parents."

Even then I recognized the significance of that moment. I raced my bike home feeling as if it floated over the pavement. I had been issued a passport to another country, a life of my own making. I didn't realize it then, but reliving my life now, I realize I had long since begun to detach myself from my family and was feeling guilty. Perhaps there was some mystery I didn't understand; perhaps their unethical behavior was somehow rational on an adult level I didn't yet understand, maybe responsible, even virtuous; perhaps I was a bad boy even to question their behavior. But now Dr. Bartlett had spoken. I could dream without guilt, travel the National Geographic maps of the Arctic thumbtacked to the ceiling above my bed, imagine my war, make up a life of writing stories, or even become an artist.

I am fascinated by those moments such as the one in Dr. Bartlett's office on which my life turned.

That turning point was positive, but another seemed negative at the time. Now I think it was also liberating. I forced myself out of my natural shyness so I could serve Jesus Christ, took elective public speaking in high school and even served in my senior year as president of the Baptist youth group—running the Sunday afternoon meetings. I believed I could never be a pulpit minister in the Billy Sunday tradition of grand gestures, Bible pounding, and platform pacing to which I was brought up, but perhaps I could be a minister who wrote or somehow did good work behind the scenes.

But there was a secret problem. I was having trouble believing in the white Republican mill owner God of my family who lived in a big white wooden house with a curved driveway and made explicit decisions for each of us, justifiably killing, for example, my Aunt Helen who died as a nurse in the flu epidemic before I was born because she had dated a man who had once smoked or drunk a beer, perhaps both, before he was converted. Again and again my grandmother and my mother told me that our God had saved my aunt by killing her in the flu epidemic and that she waited happily in Heaven to meet me.

I accepted that this God ruled my life. He—and of course God was then a He—terrified me, but I thought that was appropriate. In a fire-and-brimstone religion, the fear of God was expected. He loved me, I was told, but it was a harsh love filled with the possibility of smiting. My father and Uncle Will stood in for Him when they smote me with the leather shaving strap, and Mother did her best with the back of her bone hairbrush, wetting it so it would hurt more. They disciplined me in God's service.

I didn't question God's reign of terror for many years, but doubt, which is essential to true belief, came with increasing maturity. I began to wonder about practical questions: where did they put all the people in Heaven; how did they build the mansions that my grandfather Morison Smith had prepared for Grandma; how did Jesus, who looked Jewish and was, have a father who looked New England Republican; and how did He have the time to monitor me night and day, giving me the sniffles and growing warts on my palm, when He had so many other sinners to monitor? I suffered alone with my doubt knowing He read my mind. I prayed at night, in class, on my bike, in church but got no answers.

Finally, I shared my doubts with my pastor. He did

not take me seriously, assuring me that I was a big guy and that the women in the congregation would admire me, and that I would raise a great deal of money as a minister. This horrified the shy, introverted, aggressive, idealistic seventeen-year-old I was at the time.

I went to a youth minister who was closer to my age, thinking he would understand. He gave me the same answer and so did a third minister. It became clear to me that they had never addressed their own doubts. Consequently, when I went off to Tilton to college, I went to one church the first Sunday, another the next, and by the time I had attended each of the many churches in that small New Hampshire town, my connection with organized religion was over. The turning point had passed.

I was never angry at those ministers, then or now, just sorry for the lives of unresolved doubts they were living, and when I became a teacher, I promised myself I would never brush aside a student's question no matter how uncomfortable the answer, in conference or class, might make me feel.

I often thought of a turning point that took place when I was about thirteen or fourteen and attending Camp Morgan, a YMCA camp in New Hampshire. We went on a hike across the state to the beautiful, sharp-peaked Mount Chocorua. As we started up the trail, the counselor in charge put me at the end and told me that as a senior camper, I was second in command. I loved it. I'm sure I was an officious pain. I had never been in command of anything, and second in command was a step up the ladder of life.

I have never since climbed that trail—and never will. I want no reality to diminish my experience. At one point the trail narrows to eighteen inches, perhaps twelve, perhaps six inches in my memory until it is just a toehold. On the right side a tall cliff, on the left a deep drop, perhaps a thousand feet straight down. The counselor and the first campers got across fine, but then a kid—from New York City, of course—froze in the middle. He glued himself to the wall, occasionally looking over one shoulder or the other down, down, down. He would not, could not move forward or back.

"Murray," shouted the counselor.

I looked around for who was second in command. I realized it was me. I had not been sure that I would be able to make it across when my turn came. Now I was expected to go and meet the counselor so we could pry the camper off the wall and drag him to safety. I edged forward. The camper was indeed attached to the wall. He had turned into rock.

I tugged and tugged, almost losing my balance as we pried him loose then dragged him to safety. We do not grow up in even stages. I was not the person I had been moments before. I had been called on to perform a mountain rescue. I had heard the call of duty and responded heroically.

Others have reported that this trail is wide, the cliff a slope, the drop brief, but I will hear none of it. I depended on that story to get me through World War II. It was a turning point and I had turned.

Miss Chapman, a tall, imperious, and very proper woman, knew something I didn't know when she pointed down at me in the fourth grade and commanded, "Donald, you are the class editor." Gleefully I took over and turned out a purple-inked class newspaper on the sickly yellow gelatin of what I believe was called a hectograph. I am still following her command, but I suspect the real turning point came in another experience with Miss Chapman.

In those innocent days, we visited our teachers, who all lived in the neighborhood, on Halloween to get a piece of candy each. No tricks for teachers, just enormous respect and a treat. I remember being lined up in her apartment with Herb Wheeler, Don his younger brother, and several others I cannot remember. At the moment of highest solemnity when Miss Chapman was giving each of us our single piece of candy I passed wind.

It was no half-secret squeak but the sounding of a trumpet, perhaps a tuba. I knew the world would end. God would strike me dead. Miss Chapman would tell my parents. I would never be allowed to return to school and I would remain stupid all my life. I would go to reform school.

But nothing happened. Miss Chapman finished passing out the candy. She shook my hand like she shook the others as we left. My friends broke up in uncontrolled hilarity on the sidewalk, but God did not loose lightning on me, my parents never knew, I finished fourth grade and was passed on to fifth. It was a turning point. I learned you could survive the greatest social offenses and go on.

Sometimes I think human beings learn to harden like concrete. Deep inside, I hate conflict. My instinct is avoidance, but then a conflict arises that you avoid at too great a price and your life turns according to how you respond to it. Mr. Miller had promised me a raise from fifty cents to seventy-five for the five A.M. to midnight Saturday at his market in Wollaston, Massachusetts. I now had experience. I decorated the windows, was pretty much in charge of the canned goods inventory, took orders over the phone, stacked fruits and vegetables out on the sidewalk and sold them, served behind the counter, made sausages with real intestines, even drove the delivery truck in emergencies before I had a truck license. I rehearsed my case and made my pitch for more money and he agreed—reluctantly.

As I was allowed to go home near midnight the next Saturday he gave me a fifty-cent piece. I asked for the extra quarter. He nodded no. I threw no childish temper tantrum. I found I was a little man: a nasty, scheming, tough little man.

Late next Saturday morning, at the height of business, I took off my apron and told Mr. Miller that since he had not honored my wage increase I quit. I knew he depended on me. I was certain he would concede. I walked the three blocks home and waited for him in the kitchen of our second-floor flat. My mother was horrified. Not only was she worried about the money, she was concerned with propriety. Although we lived in a working-class neighborhood, she believed we belonged across the tracks, up on the hill. We were Republicans. We admired management. We feared unions. I should respect authority. It was not proper to strike.

Then we heard Mr. Miller's huge feet that were encased in shoes and rubbers winter and summer, making his way slowly up the back steps. He knocked on the kitchen door, nodded at me in silent defeat, and we walked back to the store together—without speaking. I got my seventy-five cents and found in myself a canny toughness I had not known was there and on which I have drawn many times in the years since.

Small first steps are often turning points but we do not know it at the time. Minnie Mae sent out a magazine article of mine to *Rotarian Magazine* and a river of magazine and book publishing flowed from her belief that what I had written should not be thrown away.

When Anne, our oldest daughter, was close to graduating from the University of New Hampshire, she asked us how we planned our lives since she wanted to plan hers. We laughed and said we had not planned our lives, that it was all accident, and she became very angry, feeling that we had some mysterious access to order that we would not share with her.

Now, with an unexpected life behind her, she understands the way lives twist and turn, and I see in her what I did not see in myself but what was most certainly there: an ability to welcome change, to take advantage of the unexpected, to step from the secure, the way I stepped from an Army C-47, and relish the risks that life most certainly offers.

Chapter 5

SHAME

Let's speak about the unspeakable.

I go to the men's room and after zipping up notice a damp spot on my pants front the size of a silver dollar and growing larger. I go to the mirror and then step back until I get a full view.

Is it visible?

It is.

I try to scrub it dry but the paper towel only leaves a dandrufflike spotting that makes it worse.

I consider spattering my whole pants front with water as if I had experienced some kind of waterfall when I washed my hands. I'd done that before. It looked as if I had wet my pants and tried to cover it up.

I remember years ago going to the men's room with an elderly—about my present age—retired United States senator who was a friend of my wife's family. He was a man of enormous dignity and charm, but as we left the men's room I noticed he had a saucer-sized stain on his pants. I could see it. I could smell it and he didn't seem to notice. He shuffled forth with full Southern senatorial dignity. I swore I would never, ever be like him.

But I am.

I suffer his shame and I attempt his poise.

Someone knocks on the men's room door. A tentative rat-a-tat-tat. A pause. Knock-knock-knock. Another pause. Then one solid, demanding thud that shakes the door.

I summon the courage I once used to jump from a perfectly good airplane. After that first jump a colonel had said, "Look up," and I laughed as I saw every paratrooper had wet his pants. Then he said, "Look down."

I yanked open the door, nodded politely to the man my age pacing the floor, and marched across the huge dining room, as certain as when I went to my first dance in ninth grade that everyone was looking at me.

I strolled to the table with the false poise I had learned during a lifetime of hiding my inadequacies behind a manner, a style, a look, a walk, a way of carrying myself. I had learned to play tough boy—well, tough enough to stop being chased down alleys, to play soldier, to play newspaper reporter, to play professor. Now my ability to fake it would be tested again as I confronted a new shame.

Shame is the emotion all who are lucky enough to age must face. It begins with small things—or at least events that should be small but aren't, especially to a competitive male animal. My friend Don Graves, only six years younger but obsessed with jogging, biking, and cross-country skiing, takes the steps two at a time as I used to. I follow one at a time. He looks back down on me with pride and pity. Bob Kertzer and Michael McConnell walk ahead of me on the sidewalk, a few inches ahead. Then a couple of feet ahead, then yards. During the war I used to volunteer to be a scout and range ahead through the underbrush while the rest of the company completed their forced march on the paved road. I am not invited to help when my daughters move into their new houses. My daughters, stronger than I am, help me by doing the heavy lifting when they visit my house.

The male ego, as all women and few men realize, is a fragile thing. Years ago when I interviewed the great but physically short violinist Jascha Heifetz he made me—at six feet three inches—sit on a stool close to the floor while he sat on an abnormally high chair. But our real battle came during the bladder competition.

He'd say, "Don't you have to go to the can?"

And I would cruelly say no, knowing he had to go but could not concede that his need was greater than mine. He was a difficult interviewee, and so I kept the pressure on by refusing to say I needed to go to the bathroom as he so obviously did. I would make him get through my questions so he could go to the can. I was young and cruel. I wonder how many international crises, including wars, have been influenced by such "manly" competitions. I do know as a political, labor, and military affairs reporter that the best way to get information from a closed meeting was to stake out the rest rooms.

Most of us, fortunately, do not remember the intimate details of our toilet training, but we remember the humiliation of "accidents" once we got out into the world of playground, street, alley, backyard, and school. And we remember the cruelty bred of our self-fear that we dealt out to those at summer camp—or in infantry basic training—who wet their beds.

Shame is a dreadful emotion. I was brought up in a house of shame, given the strange and unpleasant chore of emptying my grandmother's chamber pot when I was a boy because she didn't want me or anyone else to hear her going to the bathroom at night and flushing the toilet. The chamber pot was—to her—more ladylike.

When Minnie Mae was nursing our firstborn in the other room I could not stop myself from asking Mother if she nursed me. Her answer was classic Mother: "I do not remember."

I was not surprised that she was ashamed of me when I was a child. That had been clear from the beginning. I was too fat, too thin, too quiet, too loud, too slow, too fast. My posture wasn't good, I mumbled, ate with my elbows on the table, talked with my mouth full, didn't eat my porridge, was disobedient. Later I discovered the real reason. I was the result of intercourse.

When I first heard about the facts of life, I was sitting in an old car that was up on blocks, receiving instruction from the Irish Catholic children with whom I was not supposed to play but whom I sought out because of this mystery. They knew all sorts of grown-up stuff such as where babies came from. Of course, I didn't believe them. That was ridiculous. My mother and father couldn't have done *that*. When I finally understood how we all got here—with the help of library books and pictures on pages worn with study—I realized my mother was ashamed of what she had done that brought me into the world.

I think I figured out the attraction that must have drawn my parents together, that great mystery of my childhood that grew as they used me as their sounding board about their disappointment in each other, their shame at how the other had not worked out.

My parents married late for the times. Dad was twenty-nine, Mother thirty-one. I knew they had met in Dorchester Temple, but it was only recently that I realized it was a marriage of ambition. My father, in his opinion, married up. His own mother had worked in the mills. My mother's father had run mills. My father always told me that his mother-in-law was a lady. "When she served high tea," he would begin, and then he would regale me with stories about how proper she was.

Mother must have seen in my father a man who would better himself, who would not just provide a full table, but a big house with servants to prepare the food, serve it, and clean up afterwards. It didn't work out. They spent what they didn't make and lived a life of shameful debt. My parents strangely seemed to grow beyond shame. They developed a resentment of those who, for some reason, could pay their way. It must be their ethnic background, a secret corruption, a Job-like testing by God, something. They wore masks of good breeding, behaving as if they lived in a single-family house, not in a double-decker behind an Amoco station on the trolley line.

I promised myself that I would escape their shame, owe no one when I grew up, yet I learned to hide my shame at their shame, to carry myself with a superficial poise that allowed me to become chameleon reporter, a member of whatever group I approached—and secretly, the journalist standing apart from them. In my twice-lived life I realize how I was taught by my parents to hide my shame and appear as I was not.

Then, as we age, our bodies betray us. We get up at night and sometimes we do not quite reach the john; we stop the car and run to the rest room and sometimes we do not make it. It becomes a condition of life, an elemental fear to which we have to become

accustomed—and which those of us who live with partners have to share.

This problem of the suddenly untrained personal
disposal system can create a new compassionate intimacy in a relationship. There is no hiding the situation.

"Did you make it this time?"

"Nope."

"Sorry."

When we occasionally wet the bed or, worse, leave a
trail across the floor, soil our clothes, we share this fun-
damental shame. And the sharing helps. There is no
privacy so we do what we can to help and try to turn
the shame into humor, learning what to say and what
not to say. We've each been there and will be again—
and we share the terror of a future nursing-home life in
diapers.

Despite the television commercials about devices to
deal with incontinence in an irritatingly smiley manner,
it was a long time before I scouted out the Wal-Mart
and drug store aisles for Depends and Attends and
other packages labeled with positive, euphemistic names.
Then after a while, I strolled the aisles as though I were
going somewhere else. Then one day, suddenly surprising myself, I grabbed a package, dumped it into my car-
riage, and scooted right along.

At home I fitted a "pad" into my briefs, imagining
everyone I met had X-ray eyes, and made myself sally
out into the world. Suddenly I had a new compassion

for what my wife, daughters, and all other women endure for most of their adult life—and return to as they
age. I wasn't wearing diapers exactly, more like my
granddaughter's training pants, but I did have peace of
mind. I could dribble and no one would know my
shame.

My granddaughter felt no shame at wearing some
padding. Neither would I.

Chapter 6

A L O N E N E S S

The older we get, the more we are alone. Our children have long since moved into their own lives, and the house is quiet, so quiet we can hear its own aging, the expansion and contraction of wood and pipe, the strain as the house leans against the wind, resists rain, sleet, ice, snow.

I have not gone to an office outside of the house for thirteen years. There is not the companionship of hallway and men's room and mailbox and office and, thank God, meeting room. I am on only one committee, and it rarely meets and never for more than an hour.

We do not church, club, or lodge. Once we gave big parties and were invited to big parties, then we gave small dinner parties and were invited to small dinner parties, then we had one or two people over for Sunday breakfast, but now only two or three people invite us for dinner and we try, less than we should, to take them out to a restaurant to repay them. The fact is that our bedtime now is the time when we stopped serving cocktails and invited our guests to the dinner table.

Minnie Mae has stopped going to the football games. We still go to the UNH hockey games, but rarely to concerts, plays, or even the movies. The world contracts with age. Minnie Mae no longer drives, and driving at night is not the joy it once was when I liked nothing better than to follow my headlights at top speed over hills and around curves.

I start my day with coffee and good friends, Michael McConnell and Bob Kertzer weekdays and Burgess Doherty on Sundays, then Minnie Mae and I eat lunch out almost every day and supper out more often than we like to admit. Mostly we go out alone and the trip to the supermarket is an adventure. We see doctors more than we see anyone else.

And when we are together in the house we are often apart. I am in my office, Minnie Mae in hers or the kitchen or on the enclosed porch where we sit every night, together but alone in our books and thoughts even if the television is on.

Each year we lose old friends to death or to moving away to be near their children or to enter the comfortable ghettos of the middle-class aging. We are urged to join them in Florida, Georgia, the Carolinas, Arizona, or nearby on Cape Cod, up the Maine coast, or here in New Hampshire.

My fear of aging was not loneliness but bingo. I was terrified of the loss of aloneness, of being driven to a senior center where I would confront a huge jigsaw puzzle, a class in square dancing, and find myself taking part in a community sing: "Just a song at twilight . . ."

I celebrate the loneliness of age. I like being alone with Minnie Mae and I like being alone with myself. Looking back, I am grateful for the sickly, lonely only-child-life that forced me to explore solitude, to discover how to live within my own mind, encountering worlds far greater than the horizons I could see. As I have aged I have spent more and more time alone, and that is one of the reasons these years have been the best of my life.

I sit in the restaurant across from Minnie Mae and study an elderly couple who have not spoken since they ordered. They seem strangely content with having nothing to say. There is no sign of tension between them. It is as if all has been said, shared, resolved, understood. They seem happy to be alone together.

I remember how I scorned such couples when I was young. I thought how awful it would be to become them and realize that the waitress is picking up our dishes, packing our leftover liver and onions into a doggie bag for us who have no dog, that we have eaten dinner without speaking. We are also one of those old married couples who eat wrapped in companionable silence, content to be together without speaking.

When I first met Minnie Mae I was still, in social situations, trying—if not often making it—to be what I thought others wanted me to be: one of those hale-and-hearty, outgoing, extrovert, life-of-the-party, butt-of-the-jokes, let's-liven-things-up guys. Minnie Mae didn't like this public person I energetically but ineptly played; she did seem to like the shy and serious person I tried to hide behind the public persona, the introvert whose mind left the party and did not need to speak or laugh, who shared the intimacy of silence. And I was impressed by Minnie Mae, who felt no social need to develop public and private faces, but who was always herself no matter if she was meeting a governor, old friend, new friend, family, U.S. senator, poet, minister, plumber. Minnie Mae was Minnie Mae.

Of course, there have been times in our almost forty-nine years together when I have wished that her in-your-face honesty, Popeye's "I am what I am" attitude might be tempered by a few white lies, a bit more empathy or compassion, but overall it's been great.

Minnie Mae said, early in our courtship, that to be able to live with someone, you ought to be able to live by yourself. Again she was right. Both of us were perfectly happy living alone, and so, eleven months after we met, we moved in together. In those days, that meant after marriage.

One of the great strengths of our relationship has been our aloneness. We can sit in a room in the evening not speaking. We can be alone in different rooms if not in different beds, and Minnie Mae could ride all the way from New Hampshire to Florida and back without speaking.

I cannot. I need to babble, to speak when I have nothing to say, to start the day with my cronies at the Bagelry, to reach out to people in the line at the post office, at the checkout, on the sidewalk. Most of all though, I need time alone.

I remember Professor Gwynne Daggett telling our class that an educated man was one who could be happy in a room alone. At that moment, I had a feeling of sudden illumination that a student occasionally—very occasionally—experiences during a lecture. It seemed and still seems a fine definition of an educated person, probably because it fits my nature.

My earliest memories include playing on an Oriental rug that had patterns that could become roads, cities, fortresses. I played with a cast-iron Mack truck, with the British Army lead soldiers, with the stuffed wire-haired terrier I loved, but I did not need real toys. An only child in a home of four adults, I secretly lived with a family in the wall where I had brothers and sisters, young parents, real dogs, and a life far different from mine. We often moved, and that family miraculously appeared in the walls as soon as we moved in. I knew, of course, they were make-believe. What I didn't know is that the world of make-believe, the world of the imagination would be the way I would lead my life.

I never feared loneliness. Like many only children, I was more comfortable with adults or myself than with other children. My idea of a great outing was to rise early in the morning and drive with Uncle Will to Hyannis, where he kept the books for the Hyannisport Country Club. He left me all day in the car in the parking lot where I could see the now-famous Kennedy complex. In my family's opinion, the Kennedys were not an American royal family but lace-curtain Irish who did not know their place. When I was a boy, I would certainly not have expected that I would vote for a Kennedy—or any other Roman Catholic—years later in 1960. The uncle for whom I was named ran the caddy camp at the country club and taught all the Kennedy kids to drive, an experience that confirmed his lifelong Republicanism. At that camp I heard language I never heard at home, delivered at top screech. Even Rose Kennedy cursed when a golf drive sheared off into the rough.

I would stay in the car all day with my books, a notebook in which I could draw and write, and long hours where I could step through the pages of a book and become Long John with Robin Hood in Sherwood Forest, a patch-over-my-eye pirate, a clanking knight in King Arthur's court.

I was fortunate to be a sickly child who could stay at home in bed, ignore the shouted invitations "Hey, Murray, cumonout," and lie abed reading, listening to soap operas on the radio, drawing and writing, watching the shadow dance of the maple leaves on the wall, making believe, drifting from sleep to wake and back so that the lines between night dream and daydream blurred. I missed most of second grade and had double lobar—I thought it was *lumber*—pneumonia, measles—regular and German—chicken pox, monstrous attacks of boils, whooping cough, growing pains, asthma, and every winter many attacks of bronchitis and sore throat and the flu with high fevers that caused terrifying hallucinations and nightmares. I knew I would die young—and I still think I will, since seventy-six has become young in my mind—and I still dream of the small coffin of Butler Mitchell being loaded into the huge black Packard hearse after he died of polio.

I lived as a spy in my own home, listening, far into the night, to the stories that rose through the grate in the upstairs hall or, in summer, sitting in the moist black dirt under the porch listening to the rocking, rocking, rocking and the stories that could not be told in front of children but fell between the porch boards to where I sat listening. I hid under the dining room table, behind the sofa, at the edge of doors and eventually learned that if I was quiet, I could become invisible. They would forget I was there and start telling their stories. And when I was discovered I would be sent to my room. No punishment. I had my books, the windows from which I could spy into neighbors' windows, my family in the wall, and the vast world within my head.

Of course, their hurts—except for my beatings— were done with silence, with turning away. I was not so often sent to my room where I was happy to play but, when there was a conflict or an unpleasantness, the grownups would go to their rooms and shut the doors. I learned to read the degrees of silence, the lines around the mouth, the looks, the turning away of the head or the entire body.

I am surprised, reliving my childhood in memory, how happy I was to be left alone and, once trained to aloneness, how all my best memories are of being by myself.

I remember going beyond the bounds of my block, exploring the empty house lot that had been quarried out of granite and then abandoned—it was the Great Depression—and bringing back to Grandmother the morning glories, the bachelor's buttons, the hollyhocks I found growing among the small cliffs and crevices. I liked it best when I returned alone, making up my own games, often sitting in Uncle Will's car when it was up on blocks for the winter, driving myself across the country, across the ocean.

At school I hated the classroom and feared the playground, but liked an excuse to walk the quiet, empty corridors alone. When Minnie Mae and I last moved I found a cache of high school corridor passes I finagled as school newspaper editor, stored against the terror that I might be returned to high school and made to stay in class. It was not a surprise that I found, beside the signed but blank high school passes, an equally abundant stash of yellowed army trip tickets, signed and countersigned, ready for me to fill in the blanks so I could check out a jeep and explore England, France, Belgium, Luxembourg, Holland, Germany, or Italy on my own.

In England during my war in 1944, I drove down a thin, windy road alone, going miles without seeing anyone, when I came upon a construction of enormous stones. I stopped the jeep and wandered among those unmarked stones, imagining the ancients who constructed them, what they might mean. Later I read about Stonehenge. The first night I was in Paris I did not sleep but walked the city alone.

The best times at summer camp were when I was able to explore by myself. I remember a day I spent alone searching out the waterwheel runs and cellar holes of the mills and villages abandoned in the Gold Rush less than a century before. On leave from the army, I spent the night alone on a genuine Friendship Sloop, the sailboat Uncle Don later lost in a hurricane.

I describe myself as shy, but Minnie Mae laughs. I glance in the mirrored wall at Ron's, our favorite breakfast and lunch place, and see myself working the room, shaking hands at this table, making a joke with the waitress, greeting another table, waving to a third. I'm as good at lunch as my father was at funerals, the welcoming, sympathetic deacon. Dad always knew the name and problems of the trolley car starter, Mother the name and problems of the waitress. And so do I. Minnie Mae sees me standing in line at the bank and asks me what I found out about the person ahead of or behind me. I always have a story to retell. My interest in people is not feigned, but my ability to ignite the conversation was learned. Yet, I was a contradiction. A Thanksgiving ago my daughter Hannah found me standing alone on her porch between the turkey and the pie courses, fleeing to aloneness.

The public Don Murray must be a natural me at some level, but that person was cultivated, and I was never quite comfortable in his skin. I learned to knock on the door and ask for the money for my paper route and—after several families disappeared in the middle of the night—to deny credit. I learned to wait on customers at Miller's Market. I eventually learned to teach and even, for a while, made speeches before audiences of as many as five thousand.

I became confident as a teacher, workshop leader, speaker, and even, for a time, a television host, but the greater my public acceptance, the more my discomfort increased. I was both proud of my abilities in public and suspicious of them. I did not particularly like the public self.

As I aged I found more opportunities for aloneness as distinguished from loneliness. I chose to be alone. I get up at five-thirty while Minnie Mae sleeps, delighted to walk through the lonely house alone, going out to meet my cronies for coffee at six but often being the first to leave them, looking forward to the morning alone.

One of the great delights of age is that I can turn down invitations to speak or party or visit. I can be alone with Minnie Mae or not. I can attend to that solitary part of my nature in which I am most comfortable. I am always bored in meetings, at cocktail parties, receptions, social events; often bored at dinner parties with more than six people; sometimes bored when I am with friends, even *a* friend; but never bored when I am alone. It is discomforting to admit this. Society, no surprise, wants us to be social. It has the belief that we must work in congress, and certainly there is need for teamwork and cooperative ventures, but we often ignore the importance of the individual working alone, traveling against the wishes of society, taking the unconventional path away from the road.

We want to herd our elderly into an enforced community, but Minnie Mae and I hope to escape the ghetto, to be allowed to live alone so that we can enjoy the silence, the companionship of our minds, living and reliving our lives in reflection alone together and then, if fate intends, alone.

Chapter 7

WORK

I am the person you never hear about in cardiac intensive care who says, "I wish I had spent more time at work." I am not alone. Many of us love our work more than we admit. We are defined by our work the older we get. We are the senior person in the shop or on the staff; we are the corporate or agency historian. We were the mentors for the young, the lead dog who could work harder and longer than anyone else.

The tasks we performed may seem routine or trivial to others, but we knew we were the person who kept things going. We did the job right and found in that a continual challenge and satisfaction. And as we talked retirement, we secretly dreaded it.

Everyone seems to know why people retire early, to play golf, fish, move to Florida or Arizona, but we don't understand those who keep on working, even rejecting golden handshakes. Work is more than work. Work is who we are. Work is how we survived.

When we lost our daughter Lee in August twenty-three

years ago, Dave Ellis, then academic vice president at the University of New Hampshire, offered to lower or eliminate my teaching load, to remove me from committee assignments. I thanked him but begged him to let me work full-time. I knew work would be my salvation. It had been during hard times before and it was what I counted on to get me through this loss. It was work that would make it possible for me to be a loving husband and father. I had to survive through work to help those close to me survive.

I retired at sixty-two from teaching and from campus politics not so that I could stop working but to eliminate those activities—mostly political and administrative—that kept me from the work of writing that was most important to me. I retired so I could work harder and more efficiently.

Thirteen years after my retirement and my heart attack, I have my daily word count for the past three years on my bulletin board. Actually my annual word-count charts go back decades. Laugh if you want, but Faulkner, Hemingway, Greene, Trollope, and many others counted words. Many people see writing—painting, playing music, acting, dancing, composing—as magic, a matter of inspiration and talent, but the arts are, above all, work, just plain old-fashioned, show-up-early-every-morning, get-your-butt-in-the-chair work. A lifetime habit.

My work is writing, but if it were not, I would keep

working. I would bag groceries, get a job in a bookstore, drive a taxi part-time, become a security guard, find some work I could do that would get me up in the morning, give order and purpose to my day. It is not the romance of writing that is my first seduction, but the attraction of work itself.

The Victorian novelist Anthony Trollope, in his *Autobiography*, wrote:

> As I journeyed across France and Marseilles, and made thence a terribly rough voyage to Alexandria, I wrote my allotted number of pages every day. On this occasion more than once I left my paper on the cabin table, rushing away to be sick in the privacy of my stateroom. It was February, and the weather was miserable; but still I did my work.
>
> It has . . . become my custom . . . to write with my watch before me, and to require from myself 250 words every quarter of an hour. I have found that the 250 words have been forthcoming as regularly as my watch went.
>
> There are those who would be ashamed to subject themselves to such a taskmaster, and who think that the man who works with his imagination should allow himself to wait till inspiration moves him. . . . To me it would not be more absurd if the shoemaker were to wait for inspiration, or the tallow-chandler for the divine moment of melting. . . .

A man can always do the work for which his brain is fitted if he will give himself the habit of regarding his work as a normal condition of his life. I therefore venture to advise young men who look forward to authorship as the business of their lives, even when they propose that that authorship be of the highest class known, to avoid enthusiastic rushes with their pens, and to seat themselves at their desks day by day as though they were lawyer's clerks; —and so let them sit until the allotted task shall be accomplished.

It is easy to ridicule Trollope's statement, calling it anal, obsessive-compulsive—give him a Prozac, give him a couple dozen Prozacs, tell him to chill out, get a life. Well, he had a life. I can't tell you what a comfort those paragraphs were to me when I first read them.

I knew how to work—bike a newspaper route, drive a grocery truck, deliver a message through enemy lines, pass a lit course, write to deadline. Early on I knew how to work. I didn't know if I had the talent to be the writer I wanted to be. I did know that it was hard work to make writing come easy, but I could work as Trollope's lawyer's clerk. I could plant my rump in the writer's chair and keep it there "until the allotted task shall be accomplished."

In our society we speak openly about sex, body parts, mental and emotional ailments, relationships, money, religion, politics. I do, myself, although I was brought up in an age of discretion, reserve, dignity, formality, and privacy. Even I worry that there is no such thing as intimacy. But we still have secrets.

Work habits are the first secret. It is not contacts that brings success but work. The early bird does get the worm. Come in early and stay late. Learn your trade. Pay your dues. And if you do, you may well love your work.

I will never forget Mr. Miller assigning me to make his special Scots beef sausage in the back hallway of his tiny store. I remember the great tub of meat, so ice cold it hurt my fingers, and the secret ingredients— mostly salt—and the coils of sausage and the long learning it took to mix the meat by hand, feed the intestines on the tube, pound the sausage meat into the top of the machine with my right hand while feeding out the intestines with my left hand, twisting each sausage at just the right plumpness and length. Mr. Miller did not give praise, but I got a nod and was assigned again and again after school to make more sausages. It was work, a craft I mastered, and it gave me as much satisfaction as a poem or this page.

We don't admit that secret love of work, the task accomplished. We grump along with our fellow work- ers, but across the country many who are eligible for retirement keep on working. They have to be bribed to quit—or be downsized. As we become healthier in our sixties and seventies, more and more of us continue to work.

Work is our virtuous evasion. For as long as we have walked upright, men have fled marital conflict, parental contradiction, family confusion by leaving the cave to hunt—or the house to go to the office. Now women in our society are tasting the pleasures of such virtuous evasion. The office is where we have control—the task assigned, the task attended, the task completed. We have lists, priorities, plans and planners, deadlines, flowcharts, rituals, and order.

Golf, fishing, gardening, remodeling, boating, motor-homing, bird-watching, and other activities keep many happy in the last third of their lives—because they make their play, work. They labor hard to scrape the boat bottom, work as hard to lower their golf score as they once worked to increase their sales record. I am astonished by the work-driven compulsions of those who play their way through retirement.

As I age, I avoid the hard work of play, finding the familiar work of writing an increasing consolation. There are the obvious satisfactions in work. I found that when I brought money home as a boy I was treated differently. I was a potential financial resource to my parents. My two-bit or sometimes four-bit affluence gave me power, respect, independence. I wasn't a kid. I was a moneymaker.

It is as true today. I'm still bringing home a buck although my beard is white, my hip stiff, my hand shaky. I'm not yet dependent. Not yet.

In fact, work is power. When I work I am still in the game, my poker chips are in the pot, and as a writer, I may be heard. I don't expect agreement, praise, change of mind from my readers, but I take deep satisfaction in being heard. There is an important "I" quality to work. It is who I am. In our society, we constantly ask people who they are, identifying—and classifying—them by their jobs. It may be a funny way to run a society but we rarely answer the question by saying parent, friend, lover, helper, mentor, companion, although we probably should. Instead we say detective or lawyer or sales rep or engineer or manager or doctor or businessperson. I say writer, which makes some people uncomfortable, but it gives me pride. My wife noticed that I never called myself a writer even after a Pulitzer until, in my forties, I found myself categorized as such in an English department, a status that stood apart.

The true satisfactions of work run far deeper than money or status. Each year of my aging, I more deeply appreciate the satisfactions of work. First is the challenge. The sculptor Henry Moore said:

> The secret of life is to have a task, something you devote your whole life to, something you bring everything to, every minute of the day for your whole life.

And the most important thing is—it must be something you cannot possibly do!

The terror of the blank page must be there. Whatever your work, I think you need the contradictory feelings of terror and confidence. It must be like the
world-class skier heading down the slope, flying down
the alp between danger and competence. Each morning I come to my writing desk with the same contradictory feelings: I am fearful I will not be able to write well
enough; I am also confident that I will be able to write
well enough. Without the real terror, it would not be
worth the effort; without the confidence, it would not
be possible.

Those of us who love our work and refuse to give
it up as we age experience a continual learning. We
learn the tricks of our trade and then we have to
unlearn them. We can be the prisoner of competence
and so we have to keep challenging our craft. When
I taught, I identified what had worked best in each
course the previous semester and eliminated it the
next. In that way, I gave myself a new challenge—and I
also learned about teaching; moving, for example, from
teaching skills to increasing the emphasis on attitude,
from telling my students to listening to them, from
commanding to observing, from instructing to becoming a monitor of my students' own learning.

I write journalism and poetry, fiction and nonfiction.

I write, for example, columns that are all in dialogue or narrative, are humorous or serious or a combination of both, relieving the solemnity of one column with humor, putting a humorous column in context with a touch of solemnity.

I consider myself, after sixty years of publishing, an apprentice to my craft. I treasure what the famous Japanese artist Hokusai said:

> I have drawn things since I was six. All that I made before the age of sixty-five is not worth counting. At seventy-three I began to understand the true construction of animals, plants, trees, birds, fishes, and insects. At ninety I will enter into the secret of things. At a hundred and ten, everything—every dot, every dash—will live.

The work of writing is my therapy. As I write, defining and describing my fears and joys, anxieties and satisfactions, I begin to understand them and reduce the terrors to the manageable. It is the unknown that truly terrorizes. Each visit to the hospital—so far—is less frightening because I have been there before. I know the territory. In writing I visit and revisit my life, living it again, and every time seeing what I did not see before.

Those of us who love our work find it filled with surprise. There is always the unexpected. I write what I do not know I knew. This is the secret of the artist: We do not know what we are doing until it is done. Seventy-five or twenty-five, our craft takes us beyond plans, goals, expectations. We fail and the failures are instructive. We write what we do not mean to write and find a meaning greater than we could have dreamt.

Work is our play. I can still remember playing with blocks or with my lead soldiers on the living room rug or coloring in a book or organizing my stamps or building a tower with my Lincoln Logs or Erector set or reading, passing from this life into the world of story, and jumping when someone spoke. I have been lost to the world in the concentration of play. And as we get old, as our imaginary fears become reality, as we make appointments with yet another specialist, wait for the results of yet another test, I still know the blessing of concentration, of work. Minnie Mae comes down to my writing desk, speaks, and I jump, leaving my chair, shaking as I fall back down to my seat. I have not been where I appeared, an old man at work, but had escaped into the country of work, where all my attention is focused on the task, the solving of a familiar problem that has become wonderfully unfamiliar in its doing.

Chapter 8

S T U F F

As we age, the stuff that surrounds us multiplies—and becomes invisible. When we were young, we were disgusted with what our parents did not see: their stuff, the dust on the stuff, the stains on the wallpaper, the worn spots in the rug, the teacup edges grown brown with a hundred thousand sippings. We marveled at how age made their stuff invisible to them. Now, when our daughters visit they try to clean or toss what we haven't seen—but still try to protect. It's *our* stuff.

Now, eight times a day, a dozen, more, I make my way to or from my office, which extends out under our back porch at the farthest corner of the basement. I weave my way through stuff I did not see until I wrote the last paragraph and decide it is time for anthropological research. On the top of the heap in the middle of the floor is the seat of my old office chair upside down, the shaft broken from the base that sits under it right side up. The framed print of Picasso's *Don Quixote* we no longer hang, a camp stove we have never used, the small trunks we bought in London to ship home stuff we bought on our extended visit there in the early 1970s, the antique trunk Minnie Mae intended to refinish in the 1960s, wooden boxes and cardboard boxes and plastic boxes—some empty and some full—the plastic filing systems that I expected to use to bring order to my office but didn't, a plaster bust made by Anne when she was an art major in the early '70s, junglelike vines of wires that sent power to the lights Minnie Mae used to start plants during New Hampshire's long, late winter for the vast vegetable gardens she no longer plants, baskets that brought gifts but couldn't be thrown out when they were empty. Stuff.

Along one wall, shelves with dusty suitcases—three-suiters, two-suiters, one-suiters, and overnight cases; coolers, metal and plastic, little and large; Christmas wrappings and decorations. Stuff.

More stuff. Tools bought for one bungled job and discarded. I can't name them anymore. My jump boots hung by their laces and my hockey skates from 1939, not worn in at least sixty years. Canes and crutches, batteries with no charge, insulated mugs, mysterious bags of stuff. I open one. It is a plastic bag filled with plastic bags.

The sewing room, where my daughters would go after school or work and run up a dress for that night's party, has two idle sewing machines and heaps of material, folded and rolled up and unrolled and draped and piled and alped, spilling from table and floor, decorated with tissue pattern paper. Stuff I usually do not see.

On another wall and around the corner, shelves upon shelves of canned tomatoes, vegetable juice, jellies and jams, pear honey, and chili sauce, most jars filled with black, aged stuff, some dated in the 1950s, some moved from Wellesley, Massachusetts, to Glen Ridge, New Jersey, in 1953 and then, ten years later, taken to New Hampshire. I look at the jars and see Minnie Mae and her mother, who then lived with us, working together at the heaping piles of grapes or tomatoes or peaches, cabbages for sauerkraut, working far into the night, hear the pop of the jars sealing in the kitchen as we lay in bed upstairs.

Most of the stuff, however, does not bring memories. It irritates. It moves when I am asleep, making the aisle I follow to my office narrow—and narrower. We do get rid of stuff, generation upon generation of computer boxes we were told to save. When they almost reached to the ceiling they went to the dump, but the pile breeds, stuff giving birth to stuff.

It is a wonder how we accumulate. We don't buy doodads and figurines. We go to Europe and return with carry-on luggage and not a single souvenir. We don't do shops; we don't decorate. Minnie Mae never buys on impulse; I buy only books and CDs on impulse. We are not stylish. I bought my last suit—which

I wear only to weddings and funerals—in 1971; Minnie Mae often brags that she is wearing a blouse, a skirt, a dress that she owned before we married forty-nine years ago. Yet we have stuff in closets and stored away in trunks and almost-never-opened chests of drawers and in drawers under our king-size bed. And stuff on top of dressers and along the edge of the stairs leading to the second floor, on the dining room table and the porch table on which we eat, on coffee table and sofa and shelf and floor. Without any noticeable effort, we accumulate.

We are not, however, owned by our things, forever dusting and polishing, ordering and reordering them. They just sit where we have put them down. They are not a burden unless we want to use the table or the sofa, and then we move them, placing them on top of what we moved the last time company came. But from time to time the piles become suddenly visible and one of us will say, "We've got to get rid of this stuff."

I dream of a Japanese home, an almost empty room decorated with a single flower in an exquisite pot on a black lacquered table. My desktop is usually neat, the chaos hidden from view. Minnie Mae works in a compost of papers that swirl across her desk, up on the boxes at the back of it, flowing to the small tables on each side of the desk and down to the floor. A friend, attempting kindness, said our home has the lived-in look.

We have given away as many as 2,200 books in one swoop, but books still are piled on shelves, table, sofas, the floor. The hall closet is jammed with unworn coats, huge goose-down parkas, plastic jackets, raincoats, a fur coat, denim jackets, stuff never worn, and above, on two shelves, hats—cowboy and northeaster slicker, goose down and polar, tweed and canvas—and caps, dozens and dozens of caps with logos from schools and organizations and conferences I no longer remember.

My closets are filled with clothes I will never wear and those I do pile up on a cedar chest and chest of drawers. I open a drawer. It is filled with old watches, glasses through which I could not see, wallets without money, cards to what I do not know, my old military police whistle. I slam shut the drawer. Stuff.

Every once in a while I make a serious suggestion that we should imagine we are dead and move to a motel so our daughters could come, as they will have to some day, and clear out the stuff. I laugh but nobody thinks it funny. I don't either. I am serious.

I'd like to think we are nostalgic, saving our past in objects packed with memory, but we are not very sentimental, not in this way. Our memories arise from our living, rarely from things. We are the victims of inertia—and our genes.

Minnie Mae's family in Kentucky was Ohio River German and poor. They cooked and ate parts of the pig that I didn't know existed. They mended and patched and made do. It was heroic and successful, and necessity became a way of life. When Minnie Mae's mother, Katie, came to live with us she made soap—some is still in the basement. One day we noticed that above our sink there was a line of glasses—glasses for old-fashioneds and whiskey sours and Scotch or sour mash on the rocks (it was the 1950s). We spied on Katie and discovered that when a glass came back to the kitchen with unmelted ice cubes, she saved them. She drank the water from saved ice cubes rather than waste water by turning on the faucet.

It is hard for Minnie Mae to toss anything out, old food or old clothes. Her saving ways, she reminds me, have made it possible for me to retire and continue to eat. She is right, but uncontrolled virtue can become a problem. You can save only so much in a ten-room house.

Her genes clash with mine. I know all the jokes about Scots frugality, but I am pure Scot and my relatives are generous to a fault. My folks spent more than they earned. They gave it away. If a playmate liked a toy or sweater of mine, I was told to give it to them. I learned to hide the toys I didn't want to lose. While Katie saved, my mother tossed out. Our flats were barren, impersonal as the hotel rooms she wished were her home.

We are trying to get rid of stuff, but it is hard. I pick

up a book or a jacket to toss and Minnie Mae's genes
ask, "Have you read the book?" or "Isn't there still wear
in it?" and then I feel as if she has again attacked the
wasteful habits of my parents and, of course, I get mad
and . . .

Something has to be done. Still, my favorite knife is
the paring knife passed down in Minnie Mae's family,
worn by use and resharpening until it is a thin stiletto
blade that bends in use but can edge the wedges of
grapefruit with a feline grace.

When the stuff becomes visible, I think of the cul-
tures where the dead were buried with weapons, tools,
riches, and comforts for a journey to another world. I
wonder if I would want that knife buried with me. No,
I don't think so, but it is an interesting question. What
would I choose? Not family pictures. I don't carry photos
of Lee, the daughter we lost, or my parents, my children and grandchildren. The pictures lined up throughout the house spark memories, frozen in time, but the
pictures in my mind are active, alive, ever changing. I
am assuming that memory will travel with me wherever
I go. What things do I need?

My dozen favorite suspenders? The back scratcher
Grandma used to extend her reach during her bedridden
life? My morris chair? My collection of Bach cantatas,
the CDs I play at the start of most mornings? Books—
poems by Eamon Grennan, Sharon Olds, Jane Kenyon,

Mary Oliver? Shakespeare, Tolstoy, or a few mysteries to help me escape the boring travel through darkness?

No. I'd travel with as many blank pages as the boat-man who ferries me across the River Styx allows: the three-by-five lined Levenger cards I carry in my slim shirt-pocket briefcase; the National spiral daybooks, eight-by-ten with narrow-ruled, greenish Eye-Ease paper; the Canson Field Sketch Book, five-by-seven; and boxes of Sanford Uni-Ball Grip pens with black ink and a fine point. These are what I carry with me from office to porch to grocery store and post office and restaurant. As the blank pages fill, they reveal my life—and what I think and feel about my life. I would miss them the most.

Not my computers, not my books and CDs, not all the stuff that is piled at the edge of my vision, just page and pen that provide the daily surprise.

Chapter 9

F E A R

As we age we talk more freely about death than our children want us to. We may say who should inherit what, what kind of service we want, where we keep the living will, and how we do not want to be kept alive as a vegetable. I say I refuse especially to be broccoli, in an effort to lighten the topic. It doesn't.

But please allow us, children, to talk about what makes you uncomfortable. It is one way we deal with the inevitable. We need to talk about our not wanting to end up in a nursing home, whether we want cremation or burial, when to pull the plug. Denial works only so far, then reality, usually in what happens to friends or neighbors of our own age—or younger—strips away the illusion of immortality.

Sometimes our reactions contain a certain black humor. I remember how chilled I felt when my mother-in-law, who lived to ninety-six, read the obits from her hometown paper and gleefully, almost gaily, reported she had outlived an old neighbor. Now, however, I turn to the obit page of *Foster's Daily Democrat*—a fiercely Republican paper—each afternoon, then go back to page one. At seventy-five closing on seventy-six, I don't feel her gleeful accomplishment, but I am aware of how many die who are younger than I am. I may even come to feel Katie's sense of cruel glee one of these afternoons.

On my mother-in-law's last visits, she'd give a quilt or a ring to her daughter or a granddaughter and talk almost casually about when she would "go." We tried to change the subject—which irritates me when my children do it. My mother-in-law never, however, talked about her fear of death.

I suspect she did not fear death. She feared that lightning would strike an air conditioner, so she would not have one installed when she returned to live in Kentucky. She feared that someone would break into her home, so all the windows were closed and locked all summer long. She feared that women who she thought did not know the way of the world would report the news on television and to her horror, they did. She hesitated to go downtown, fearing in her nineties that some young handsome black man would rape her. We were both outraged by her racism and amused by her apparent belief in her sexual attractiveness. But the fear was, unfortunately, real to her, and she would not go out alone in her last years, a prisoner of the crime fears that terrorize so many elderly people.

The grandmother with whom I lived was bedridden much of my life, and I was closer to her than to my parents, but she never admitted the slightest fear of death. My own folks, in their turn, seemed to welcome death. Father, after a series of heart attacks and a battle with cancer he won, was not happy in his life with Mother—never had been as far I could tell—and when he was unable to escape all day and most nights to business or church, the tension became worse. In fact, the hospital staff, having met her and seen her effect on my father registered on cardiac monitors, suggested he go to a rest home, not return home. He felt obligated to live with Mother, sure it would limit his days, and it did.

Mother, free of my father at last, lost all reason to live and kept hoping for her own "release." She was gone in less than two years.

As a matter of fact, I don't remember any of us admitting our fear of death in combat. Perhaps it was just the macho-paratrooper image we tried to maintain, or perhaps, after our first skirmish, it was an acceptance of our own inevitable death. But I do remember moments of gut-emptying terror under fire and the private, never-once-shared struggles I had before a jump, even the rumor of a jump, or before we returned to the front or, at the front, when we heard the first sounds of shells pouring down or the rustles in the woods that signaled another enemy attack.

Fear, even if unspoken, is the shadow companion of aging. It seems to me to be less and less the fear of death itself. Although I am certainly not ready for that last adventure, there are plenty of other fears to go around. The first fear is dependence. Last night I found myself on a low footstool with knees that refused to hinge on order. I called for Minnie Mae, who is more than a foot shorter and more than a hundred pounds smaller than I am. She gave me a hand and I found myself upright.

It is fair enough. Many times a day I have to help her out of a chair, up or down a step or curb, across an uneven walkway. Balance is the most obvious symptom of her Parkinson's. I have been instructed in helping her by the way in which she, once a fiercely independent woman, has accepted a creeping, insidious dependence.

It took us a long time to escape our childhood and make our own way in the world. It also took us a long time to decide what way in the world we wanted, but finally we have matured. We have escaped the rule if not the haunting of our parents; we have found our way to jobs and families and friends and service; we have escaped at last from ambition, from duty and obligation, and from the tyranny of what others will say. We have become, if not content with ourselves, accepting of ourselves.

Then the fear of dependence surfaces. I visit with

Anne or Hannah and their families. I like my sons-in-law and my grandchildren, but at the moment of greatest contentment, I feel a chill. I see myself not as a visitor but as the old man living upstairs who needs caring, perhaps help to the john, meat cut up on his plate, a polite ear for a story I tell again and again and again. They will be kind, but I will be aware of their pity.

I play out the drama of dependence every day. Minnie Mae was a substitute blind date, and when I called on her the next night, it was Valentine's Day and I brought her a small spice rack, since I had suggested taking her out to dinner and she had said she would cook in. She was furious. She did not like presents. Whether she felt unworthy or simply did not want the obligation implied by acceptance, I have never been sure. Perhaps both are true, but the message was clear: Don't buy me dinner, I'll cook; don't bring me presents, I can't be bought.

Next to dependence is the fear of loss of dignity. Minnie Mae has shown me that dependence does not mean loss of dignity. Many times she is accosted by excess help. When I give her a hand, she does the lifting. She is in charge. Most people grab and yank. They are in charge. Minnie Mae is startled, but instead of being angered, she realizes their good intentions and thanks them with a smile, later grumping to me.

Of course, our ultimate fear is that simple physical

dependence and some help with the checkbook and paying bills may progress into the many forms of mental deterioration we group under Alzheimer's. You do not age in our society without seeing close friends or relatives—bright, clear-eyed, and clearheaded men and women—deteriorate. As a friend of mine whose father had just died of a series of fatal physical ailments said, "Through it all, Dad was Dad." But his mother suffers from Alzheimer's and he says, "Mother is no longer Mother."

Every time we forget a name, a place, the reason we have gone to the other room, we have a quick, rapier stab of worry. We reassure ourselves by saying that if you forget where you left the keys, it isn't Alzheimer's. However, if you forget what a key is, then . . .

If you can no longer drive in a wheel-dependent society, if the pot burns on the stove, if you can no longer remember when to take your pills—or which pill to take—then you may have to be put away. "Be kind to your children," a friend advises, "they will choose the nursing home."

Minnie Mae and I not only have the normal terror of the nursing home—we see ourselves sitting gap-mouthed, tipped to one side in a wheelchair, stuck in the corridor for an afternoon or more—we have almost as much fear of the upper-class ghetto, the retirement community where I would only be with people of my age or older, of similar religious, educational, socioeconomic backgrounds, a place where I would be expected to dress for dinner, wear socks, eat the same food with the same people, talk the same talk of who was failing, who had been moved to assisted care, to full care, to the cemetery.

Few of us, I think, are afraid of dying. In combat, I accepted my death and went on, not worrying about it. I worried about revealing my fear, having a task I could not do, failing my comrades, breaking down, suffering a crippling wound. It is the same way in the Battle of Age.

I have come to the far edge of life where I experience a calm acceptance and a great curiosity. I do not want to leave and am glad still to be here, but when the time comes I hope I do it well, slipping quietly into the final sleep as did the grandmother I hardly knew. At eighty-nine she was really sick for the first time in her life. She had the tuberculosis she had contracted as a girl working in a mill, which lay in ambush for seventy years or more. Now she also had pneumonia, which we used to call the old woman's friend.

I stood alone with her, holding her hand as she struggled to breathe once more, then after a while, once more, and then the pain left her face. She smiled and was gone.

I hope I will as gently smile.

Chapter 10

LIFTING

When I was a boy I didn't exercise, I just ran everywhere and played games, stickball, vacant-lot baseball and football, church league basketball, street and ice hockey. I dreamt of becoming Jimmy Foxx and playing first base for the Red Sox or turning into Frankie Brimsek, goalie for the Boston Bruins hockey team. But I didn't lift or stretch or push, I just played.

School sports were pretty much out for me. I did play goalie on the North Quincy High School soccer team in the ninth grade, but most of the time I worked after school and weekends. I didn't even try out for teams. A dream did come true when I was given a football scholarship as well as money as a dormitory floor director at Tilton Junior College. I played right tackle in 1942 when no substitutes were allowed to return to the game, and so I stayed on the field after banging up the right knee that still hurts in the year 2001. The next few years I exercised in the paratroops, but when I came home I did what most men, especially of the lower classes, did in those days: I gave up exercise. No games for me, I was grown up; no golf in silly plus fours, no tennis in white underpants. We were men and we behaved like men, growing pear shaped as proud evidence of our ability to put red beef and mashed potatoes on the supper table.

When the exercise fad began I thought that anyone who had time to play tennis or golf or sail or swim or hike or jog or bike clearly was not doing their job. Had I been an executive I would have looked on anyone who exercised as being lazy, not giving work appropriate priority. With lower-middle-class snobbery I would have seen them as Ivy League aristocrats, playboys and playgirls, not to be taken seriously in their sporting outfits. Had I been the owner of a corporation, I would have thought taking time to exercise would be just cause for dismissal.

Besides it wasn't dignified. When grown persons started jogging past our house in their underpants, I giggled. When I knew them, I unleashed ridicule. I thought them narcissistic, displaying an unhealthy and probably perverted or onanistic interest in their own bodies. I had read the Boy Scout handbook and knew that was bad. I was embarrassed and more than a little uncomfortable when more and more neighbors and colleagues jogged past all sweaty and wearing under-wearlike garments in public. Some took to bikes and tight-fitting, long shorts. I imagined their smugness—well, it may not have been imagined. And when a friend bought a bicycle and came by in funny shoes, skintight pants, a color-coordinated T-shirt, strange biking gloves, and a helmet with a tiny rearview mirror, I tried to suppress my giggles, but failed. When he left I doubled over with great heaves of laughter.

On the advice of doctors and the uninvited lectures of exercise converts, Minnie Mae and I joined a heart group that walked around a gym with another group of people who were disgustingly cheery before six in the morning. That didn't last. I walked for a while with two early morning coffee companions until their schedules changed. We bought two exercise bikes and one tread-mill; they hung with laundry in the bedroom then were gotten rid of. And we visited health clubs where the young mate. There we witnessed the most ridiculous exercisers of all—weight lifters.

My friend Chip Scanlan started lifting weights. I laughed, I howled, I needled him and, off the phone, said more critical things to Minnie Mae. Weight lifting! How silly can he get. As I went on—and on and on—developing a routine of ridicule about those who lifted weights, I should have known. I said I would never get married—and I did, twice. I said I would never work on a newspaper—and my first job after graduation from college was on a newspaper. I said I'd never go to New York City—and was working there within six weeks. I said I'd never teach—and became a professor. I said I'd never lift weights.

The doctors kept the pressure on. Minnie Mae's Parkinson's, my heart problems, our diabetes made exercise a necessity. Still we resisted—for years. Then Minnie Mae read *Strong Women Stay Young* by Miriam E. Nelson, Ph.D., with Sarah Wernick, Ph.D., based on the study at Tufts University of elderly women who lift weights. And then she found she could not lift a few plates up onto a shelf and she got serious. She went to Synergy, a health club attached to Exeter Hospital, and I went along to support her. Minnie Mae got physical therapy, and we both were assigned a trainer who set up an exercise program on ten machines—Minnie Mae has been changed to nine—and the treadmill.

We are now those I ridiculed.

It takes time, a lot of time. Exeter is twenty minutes away when there is no traffic, and that is increasingly rare, forty minutes away when traffic is heavy. It takes us about two hours to get in, changed, exercised, showered, and out. Afternoons disappear.

But it is amazing for me to watch Minnie Mae, who claims she is still five foot one, chug along the treadmill or toddle from weight machine to weight machine. Minnie Mae, with her Parkinson's, osteoporosis, and problems with depth perception, lifts up to 17,000 or more pounds a week and is shamelessly proud of her new muscles at eighty-one years of age.

I'm constantly amazed at what we can do—and at

the science of exercise. In some ways I think I am in better condition than when I played football or ran from Germans who were shooting at me. Certainly I feel I have more upper-body strength. Our training more than fifty years ago on the football field and in the military was endurance and mind games: could you take it? I could take it, but I was never very strong. I am now. For my age, for my health, I am proudly strong.

I find I am ridiculously competitive. Minnie Mae, a woman, lifts to her own measure. Don, the male, sneaks a look at what other males lift. He laughs when he puts a proud 240 pounds on the leg press and finds the man before him has done 350, but there are few joys better than seeing a young man sweat on the lat pulldown and find he has been straining at 70 pounds for two sets while I do 130 pounds for a set of twelve. I have not yet beat my chest and roared out loud, not yet.

And more embarrassing, I have discovered those endorphins that I had scorned more than the costumes of public exercisers. There is a lot of stress in growing old, a lot of anxieties and worries, concerns for children and grandchildren, for spouse and friends, for the self, for the world, but when I lift I achieve the same quiet I find at the writing desk. I am lost to the world in the task, achieving a calm concentration that, yes, centers my life.

In the men's locker room at Synergy, I do hear my ancestors in Scotland laughing from their graves. I smile back and salute them as I pull on my T-shirt and shorts and Velcro-strap my sneaks. Before I punch my birth date into the combination lock, I put a pen and the case holding my three-by-five note cards into my shirt pocket. If you ask me why I carry these cards, I will admit to being a workaholic, a writer who may make a note about a future draft or add a project to my daily to-do list. Secretly, there is another reason. The inner pocket of the case carries the names of my doctors, the medications I am taking, my allergies, blood type, and who to notify if. At my age I always travel with it.

Most of the time I am comfortable with such ambivalence. I know that my energy, my zest for life, my ability to seize the day and delight in the moment are made possible by my subterranean awareness that time is fleeting. Light is made bright by dark, joy illuminated by melancholy.

As I find Minnie Mae and as we walk toward the treadmills on which we start our workouts, I remember the long walks I took with my uncles, great walkers in the tradition of our ancestors, who walked from village to village in the islands, lowlands, and highlands of Scotland. No artificial treadmill was necessary to exercise the human animal in the thousands of lifetimes that led to mine. My mother and father never exercised, but they walked. They never knew how to drive, never owned a car. They used the shank's mare.

My father, born in 1890, did not even have a child-hood, which was typical at his socioeconomic level. He was the eldest son of five children, a little man from birth, born in this country of immigrant parents who left the farmland they could never own in Scotland and indentured themselves to factory work so they could exchange an economic slavery without hope for an economic slavery in the factory that had hope. It worked.

Now I walk three times a week on an endless belt that in some ways is not unlike the loom at which my grandfather worked. I punch in my walk on the tread-mill's electronic keypad—twenty minutes one day, thirty another—that will be recorded on the Synergy computer, and I start on the FitLinxx machines that are my substitute for honest physical labor. My doctor says it is enough now to do fifteen repetitions on ab crunches, twelve repetitions each on back extensions, chest and leg presses, seated rows, lat pulldowns, tri-cep and leg extensions, and arm and leg curls for a total of 14,565 pounds.

Yes, I now get ribbed by my jogging, lifting, rowing, biking friends whom I used to ridicule. The convert is always a good target, and as I take off my clothes and head for the showers, I hear a snort from Heaven. It is another ancestor in his old kilt laughing that I had to join a club to do a good day's work. Blow it out your bagpipe. I feel good and despite the silver hair on my chest I feel young. Well, younger.

Chapter 11

A VETERAN SPEAKS

The status of World War II veterans in America has changed many times in my lifetime. We came home heroes, which I found inappropriate and discomforting. War is not heroic and those of us who survived were aware of how important luck was to our return and to those we left behind or who returned to live their years in and out of mental institutions and hospitals.

Soon, however, we were no longer heroes, just vets; a great wave of young men and women absorbed into the anonymity of civilian life. We were forgotten and most of us were glad. We tried to forget our battles and get on with the lives we had so surprisingly been granted.

Then came the almost invisible Korean War in which there were 54,246 Americans killed. The Korean War was not an unpopular war. It was just an ignored war, as if we had had enough combat, enough dying and maiming and capture and escape. It almost seemed as if we were bored with war, and those who were killed or wounded became invisible. And then the war dwindled to a stalemate. It was easy to forget, even for those of us who had served at the front only a few years before.

A generation or more later we slid into an unexpected war in Vietnam. It seemed one day we were giving advice to Vietnamese troops and the next we were at war. This war was reported in newspapers and radio in much more revealing detail than had our heavily censored war. And then there was television. The war came into our living rooms. The civilian public saw a bit of what war was like and the nation was not united. This didn't surprise our generation. The U.S. was isolationist after World War I. There were many people who did not want us to fight in any foreign war. There were even more supporters of Hitler's Germany than we like to remember, but we were united by Pearl Harbor.

There was no Pearl Harbor in the Vietnam War. There was strong opposition to the war that grew until we had to end the war and flee the country. There was public outrage as the nation began to learn that we shot civilians, that we "fragged" our own officers, that we had trouble telling enemy from friend, that we were capable of, well, war, of killing each other in every way we could imagine. Those of us who had been in combat in World War II found no new war stories. I had not gone into combat high on drugs but I had fought drunk. We had killed our officers, we had been under friendly fire, we had mistaken civilians for soldiers, had even—at times—killed for sport.

Much of the nation turned against war and then, led by Tom Brokaw, we of the World War II generation found ourselves venerated, once more treated as heroes from the good war. Of course there is no good war, but I find strangers who, upon finding out I was a paratrooper in World War II, congratulate me, tell me my generation was different and that they don't make them like me anymore. Of course they do. The boys of today could be the boys of my generation, but I hope they never have to learn to kill as I did.

As the fashions of war changed, most veterans of my generation maintained a constant silence. We did not speak of our war. There were good reasons for our silence.

In my generation, boys did not cry. If we did, we got whacked and ridiculed because we couldn't take it. We were tested at home with shaving strap, belt, open-handed slap and in backyard, playground, or alley by fist. We were expected to stand and fight, not turn tail or be yellow. Not one teacher attempted to stop the six years of recess beatings I was given because of my religious beliefs. Not one. Not in six years. They joined the ridicule of my classmates.

I learned to take it and give it. When I played sports I was never to show fear or pain. "It's bush to rub," said a baseball coach when I was hit by a pitch. Big leaguers did not rub no matter how badly it hurt. My football coach said, "Grab grass."

I spent nine weeks for each of four summers at a YMCA camp on a scholarship arranged by my uncle, who worked for the Y. I loved it, but it was a harsh environment meant to make a man of a boy. Our college-student counselors, football players mostly, punished us for minor infractions of dining room etiquette—complaining, griping, not getting along, for showing up late or early—by hitting us on the biceps with a fist with one knuckle stuck out a bit. We spent each summer black and blue from elbow to shoulder. If tears came, we got another fist. It was the era of the knuckle sandwich, the bloody nose, the cry "Four-eyes" that made any bespectacled kid like me fair game. Wear glasses and you expected to be hit.

Writing about it makes it sound worse than it was. I learned to take it, but I also learned, as the boys of my generation learned, never to show your feelings, not at home, not in school, not on the street. We were trained to silence. When I faced the harshest in-your-face drill sergeant training in the paratroops, I found it easy to accept. I was already trained not to reveal my feelings, trained perhaps not to have feelings.

When I was in the military police one of the first rape victims I had to deal with said she turned her feelings off during the rape. She had children and wanted to live. Years later, during the enlightenment of feminism, I often thought that my childhood, my schooling, my training in the Boy Scouts and at the YMCA, taught me to turn off my feelings about violence in a similar way.

Just a few years ago, a graduate student interviewed me about the war and asked, "How did you mourn?" I was stunned by the question. I didn't mourn. When fellow soldiers were wounded or killed, we took their weapons and ammo and moved forward. Our feelings were turned off. It was the way we survived.

Of course, the feelings weren't turned off. No woman raped is unaffected even if she does not resist in order to survive, and no soldier who has been under fire is untouched. Our bowels reveal our fear. But we are supposed to be men now, to come home battle-tested, bloodied, heroes of a victorious war. How can we speak of our feelings, tell what we have seen done, tell what we have done, what we have found within ourselves that is rarely heroic?

War is at best surrealistic, a landscape hard for most of us to describe. A jeep blown to the top of a telephone pole, the driver sitting at the wheel, dead. A friend holding his head in his lap, his overcoat collar surrounding a black hole. A German pissing so close I can smell it. I must breathe softly so I will not be found. A body part—a leg? an arm?—yes, I think an arm with a shoulder, arching over my head. The rain after a shell lands, after you rise up and are slammed to the ground—rocks, dirt, roots, bones, metal, blood, gravel. The sudden passage of air against your cheek. Another miss. The strange, awkward leaps of a soldier ahead of you, then another to the left, two over to the right. A minefield.

How can we sit around the supper table, describing to our children such a landscape of images that happened days, weeks, months apart? We see the body rising from the exploded mine but we don't remember seeing it fall. Perhaps it is still in the air, somewhere over Germany.

Do I put myself back where I was by the telling of a night in Belgium when I dug in and found first a uniform button, then another, then a skull? I had found a companion from a famous battle in another war. Do I make myself return to how I felt that night—the sense of comfort and companionship that that old soldier's skull gave me? Infantry combat is lonely, but that night I was not alone. I shared the waiting for the dawn attack with my personal veteran from another war. Do I want to remember when I felt comfort from a skull? Do I want to break my silence and tell it as I just have? I am not sure.

Most of all we do not remember. Much of my war is hidden in a sepia memory I cannot probe, hard as I try. I sit against a shell-shattered tree in a forest of shell-shattered trees. My rifle lies across my lap, reloaded and ready. My legs stretch out before me in the mud made warm by my body. A sergeant bends down and speaks to me. I can't remember what he said. I may have done something well or bad, I do not know, I do not know. I am alive and soon I will have to move out again.

There is more that I have forgotten than I remember about my war. Perhaps much of it has been erased. It is nowhere, the film blank. And much of what I remember may be wrong. Did I really find comfort from a skull? Did that happen, or was it in a movie, in a book, in a dream? Did I make it up? Could I really have been that crazy? Yes. I could. I was. I am sure it was not made up.

Recently John Lofty, a friend who asks good questions, asked me what it was like to live close to the earth, open to the weather night and day as I was in the Battle of the Bulge, when I sought the warmth of the huge piles of dung the Belgian farmers maintained. We walked on. I haven't yet been able to answer him because when he spoke, I was surprised by a strange nostalgia for the time when I was an animal of war, living by the rule of the sun, moving crouched over like some ancient ancestor hunter or warrior through dark woods, fearing the revealing light of the moon, taking cover at the base of trees, seeing the world as an animal does from near the ground, living in the moment, no memory, no dreams.

I am not one for nostalgia, not for childhood or school, summer camp or past careers, yet the feeling was real, for the moment, as if a door on a long-lost life opened then quickly shut. And before it shut, I saw myself sitting quite content, eating a K ration among the bodies of the dead.

If we who were there do not tell of war, the stories will be left to the historians, the novelists, the mythmakers, the moviemakers, the politicians—those old men who send boys to kill boys like themselves.

Chapter 12

WAR STORIES TOLD

I am a storyteller. It is my nature and my responsibility. I came home from war convinced that the
civilians should know that war was different than I had
been taught by history, novels, and movies.

When I returned from war in January 1946, the clan
gathered at Uncle Alec and Aunt Maud's: Ellen, my
fiancée, my parents, the uncles on my mother's side, my
cousins, Mr. and Mrs. Curtis, Aunt Maud's parents who
lived next door. After a ceremonial dinner—it must have
been Sunday and we must have had Uncle Alec's homemade chocolate ice cream—we gathered in the parlor. I
was still in uniform and cousin Malcolm, who had been
in the army but not in combat, asked how I kept my
pants bloused above my boots, knowing that paratroop-
ers used condoms to do the job. I awkwardly answered
rubber bands, and no one knew why Malcolm laughed.

I always felt uncomfortable at Uncle Alec's. I liked
him, but at a distance. He was a tall, reddish-haired
man—the result of a Viking raid on northeast Scotland

I am sure—with enormous dignity and the intimidat-
ing, almost cruel sense of humor that ran in our family.
He had married money, and these were the rich relatives who saw my father as a failure and me as a poor
relative to be shown how proper people lived. I still
have regular nightmares of being lost in that house,
mostly upstairs where there was a playroom, huge hand-
made dollhouses, a corridor of dark brown, almost black
woodwork, and closed doors I never dared open.

Now everyone's attention was turned my way. I had
to sing for my supper. They wanted a war story. Aunt
Maud had gone to Girls' Latin School in Dorchester, a
part of Boston, and had never recovered from the shock
and shame over the mayor moving into their neighborhood and his daughter, one Rose Fitzgerald, an Irish
Catholic, being admitted to her class. Yes, she became
the mother of a president named Kennedy. I had not
forgotten that my family was enthusiastically anti-Irish-
Catholic. I knew the perfect story.

"Last Easter," I began, "we were fighting our way
down a street in Germany, and when things slowed down
about noon, three of us found a safe spot, a dark corner
of a Catholic church, and broke out some K rations,
the meals you could carry in your jump pockets, you
know those baggy pockets on our jump pants.

"The sun came out and shone through where the
roof had been. It was quite lovely and appropriate for

Easter Sunday. I put down my K rations, and when I reached for another bite, my finger went down a hole." I started laughing. "I looked down. My finger was in the mouth of a dead priest." My laughter grew louder. "We were all sitting on a dead priest."

I waited for the room of Catholic-hating Protestants to join my laughter. They did not.

I suddenly realized that at twenty-one I was a stranger to those who had not been in combat, even if they were family. Of course, it wasn't funny, but if we hadn't laughed that Easter Sunday in the bombed-out church, we would have wept and been sent home with a Section Eight.

War stories and their first cousin, hunting stories, must have been the first stories. The need for narrative is as strong as the need for food, cover, sex. It is story that instructs. It is story that explains the mysterious world. It is story that manufactures meaning even when there is no meaning. It is story that puts our actions, re-actions, thoughts, imaginings, and feelings into context.

The stories are always more organized than the experience. On one jump I kept waiting for my chute to stop my tumbling fall. Usually you are slammed to a stop, but this day nothing. I looked up and my chute was a streamer, a long curling snake in the sky.

This was a defining moment. This was no imaginary terror but a simple matter of life and death, and I felt no fear, no panic, just a heightened awareness and a calm. I knew what to do and I did it.

We had a reserve chute strapped to our chests. On the ground we hadn't been able to tug it open. It was held together by a wire as thick as a pencil. They told us that if we needed to open it, it would be easy—and it was, a gentle flip of the wrist. I fed it out by hand, and it wrapped around a guy named Brown, who had jumped after me, and I became a pendulum. I looked up and saw my first chute was beginning to open a little. I reached down my right leg and pulled out the long knife we each kept there and cut myself free of Brown. We both slammed into the ground. He broke a leg.

I had looked at my watch before I jumped and I looked again once I was on the ground. Forty-seven seconds.

I didn't know if I could shoot another human being before I went overseas. Then one night in Tennessee, when I was on MP duty in a roadhouse, a bartender leaned over the sink—I can still see his bald spot, gray hair around, a long, thinnish skull—and a soldier took a brown beer bottle and smashed it into the bartender's head. The bottle didn't break, the skull did. I told my partner to see to the bartender, and I chased after the soldier. He took off across a plowed field.

I yelled at him to stop, but he kept running. I took out my forty-five, waited until his head bobbed up as he jumped a row. I fired above his head and ordered him to stop. He didn't. I waited until he bobbed up again and fired for his body. It was easy. I would have no trouble shooting at the enemy in combat and I didn't. He must have felt the wind from the bullet—a sister's kiss that I felt later in combat—and he stopped.

"You could've killed me," he screeched.

"I would have killed you. Next bullet," I snapped, cuffing him.

We don't grow older in an even march but in sudden lurches. I hadn't killed a man, but I knew then it would be easy. I was nineteen.

Many of my war stories are worn smooth with telling, yet they are a narrative of a boy changing into a soldier. I tell the story of my catching a German spy: she paid soldiers to do what they would have paid for and asked about carbines. Months later, when we passed through Washington to embark from Boston, two FBI agents got on the train, found me and took me into the train's leather-benched smoking room to thank me, and then got off in Baltimore.

Or I tell the story of working in the U.S. Army whorehouse, of crossing the Rhine with the British commandos, of being given last rites three times, each time when I was asleep under shellfire, of the huge German shell that was so slow we could see it blur past.

These war stories are taken out of experience, simplified, shaped, and then used to entertain, instruct, establish companionship, and to document whatever point in the conversation needs documentation. The stories are not the experience but a part of the experience, a moment held out of time that can be studied whenever it is needed.

War is not rational, I say. If you want to know what infantry combat is like, take a dozen twelve-year-olds on an overnight camping trip and arm them. War is confusion. I was under fire when a replacement crawled next to me in my slit trench. We were supposed to be spread out, but he stayed pressed against me all night as we took and returned fire. We had, for no reason I can explain, been armed with bolt-action, World War I British Enfield rifles. He asked, "How do you fire these?" I showed him, and he said, "But I have a withered right arm." He was a cook who was not supposed to have combat duty, but he had been scooped up and rushed to the front. He needed me and we fought as one during an unusual night of companionship in the loneliness of infantry combat, but when morning came he was gone. Killed, wounded, taken prisoner, assigned to another unit? I will never know.

I remember only one patriotic speech. A colonel before one action in the Battle of the Bulge climbed up on a chair and delivered himself of movielike statements that made some of us laugh and others so angry I thought he might be killed by one of us. Perhaps he was. It happened.

I never heard anyone pray under fire, although many

may have silently. The wounded and dying called "Medic" or "Mom." The anger I and others felt was directed not at the enemy but at our officers. We felt a strange comradeship with those whose officers and politicians had pushed us into the cockpit to fight each other. We often had brief periods of truce when we exchanged the wounded or the dead. After helping a Wehrmacht sergeant who spoke English bring one of our wounded in, I offered him coffee, cigarettes, and we chatted about his service in Africa and Italy. He actually was on leave, he said, but he could not stand being with his family during the fire bombings and had returned to the front. I offered him safe passage as a prisoner of war, and he considered it but felt he had to return, and I led him through our lines to his.

The great names of the history books were often curse words to us. Once Sergeant Guthrie and I were standing at a Y in the road when the famous General George Patton roared up in a jeep, pearl-handled pistols and all.

I had an enormous admiration for Guthrie. He was a peacetime sailor, allegedly heavyweight champion of the Pacific Fleet, who had volunteered for the paratroops and switched services, as you could during my war. Guthrie was everything in a soldier I wanted to be, and I studied his behavior carefully. Patton asked us where a specific regiment, I think the 194th, was, and we pointed to the left.

He chewed us out with a string of interwoven profanities and obscenities that impressed even me. The Germans were to the left, he claimed, shaking his map at us, the Americans to the right. I wondered what Guthrie would do. Shooting Patton seemed a fine idea to me, but Guthrie snapped to attention and gave him a sharp paratroop salute, saying, "Yessir." And I followed suit.

Now, one thing you never, never, never do is salute an officer in combat. It makes him a target for a sharpshooter. We saluted but nothing happened, and Patton went to the right in a swirl of gravel. A hundred yards away, maybe two, we heard German rifle shots and we smiled.

But then the jeep skidded back up. Now it was decorated with bullet holes. Again we saluted—go get 'im—but Patton didn't return our salute. He looked straight ahead as his driver grinned and gave us a wink.

Once, I volunteered to go north through deep snow in the Ardennes to see if I could make contact with a British unit heading south to close the pincers on the Germans. I remember the serenity of that day. I was on my own with a mission in the winter woods so like the ones I knew in New England. I had not seen any tracks, any strange movement in the woods, no sounds of metal on metal, no soldier stink, and left the cover of woods to cross a field. Six paces out and too far to return, I realized a German soldier had emerged from the woods on the other side of the field, exposed and trapped as I was. At fifty yards or so we dropped to one knee and fired directly at each other. Little blossoms of snow grew and fell around each of us, but neither of us hit the other. We did not reload but waved to each other as we passed, each continuing his mission.

Of course, we could feel hatred, especially when we had lost good men. After one such day, we took prisoners and I remember holding a rifle on one soldier who was being interrogated by one of our soldiers who spoke Russian and played to the German's fear of Russians. We had made the prisoner drop his pants, common interrogation procedure, and I watched with fascination and horror as shit crawled down his leg.

Then my assignment was changed and I was to guard more than one hundred Wehrmacht soldiers, who were lying facedown on a frozen pond, their boot toes rattling against the ice in a terrible kind of chattery clog dance. I held my rifle at my hip, and when a head raised up, I shot at it. The head went down. I don't think I hit anyone—but it was easy to shoot.

The greatest hatred I felt was against an American soldier, a buddy of mine whom I greatly liked and had known longer than most men with whom I served. This story I tell to try to make someone understand how different we become in combat.

I was sick with the flu and was taken to the battalion aid station. They took my temperature—104—and gave me a cup of some new white pills, sulfa I thought they said, and a canteen cup of black coffee and sent me back to the front. That was what I expected and it was fine with me. There was a war on and I was in it.

Then a jeep with stretchers lashed to it raced in, and two medics started fighting over the pair of jump boots with the feet still in. I thought it funny but when I got near, one of the bodies on the stretchers spoke. "Hey, Murray. I'm going back to Chicago. I got the lucky wound. You poor bastard, going back to the front."

He kept taunting me, and I saw his legs had no feet. It was his boots they were fighting over, but he kept taunting me, and when I leaned over I saw it was my friend, high on morphine. He wouldn't let up, and I felt the hate and envy rise up in me, and I started to move to choke him to death, just holding myself back until I could turn and head back to the front, full of sulfa and rage and fear, not so much of the enemy but of myself.

Are you surprised we are so often silent?

Chapter 13

WAR STORIES UNTOLD

Despite such war stories I have told myself and others, I had not thought my war central to my life. It was something to survive and put behind me. During my childhood, I had seen what I called professional veterans, many who had never been under fire, parade on Memorial Day and the Fourth all dressed up in uniforms that never quite fit. I thought them silly, men and women who lived in the past. I would not be one of those barroom heroes telling the same stories over and over again, reliving moments of glory that were not glorious, no bands and banners at the front.

But as I have aged, I have heard myself tell my war stories and I have begun to realize how much the war is still with me. It is not often the topic of conversation with my psychiatrist—my childhood is—but I have come to realize that few of us who fought are ever discharged from our wars.

I unscrew the cap on the carton of ruby red grapefruit juice this morning and find a plastic ring. I put my right index finger in the ring and give a quick tug. My hand remembers a grenade, a ring pulled free with my left index finger, how this right hand held the grenade tight, the arcing toss, more like a shot put than a pitch, the explosion, a scream.

I pour my juice and notice my hand does not tremble as it so often does these days. Perhaps my hand is nineteen and still back in combat.

My time travel began when I woke, still half wound into a dream that fades into brown sepia shapes, then disappears before I can make it out. It must have been of my secret war, the one with the stories untold, because my legs move as if I again crossed a minefield. When I piss in our toilet bowl, steam rises from snow in the Battle of the Bulge; when I wash my face, my hands cup themselves to scoop up the water I have slurped from my canteen into my helmet as I learned to do during those days in the field and still do this morning, so many, so few years later.

When I came home from my war, surprised to be alive, I don't remember joy but a kind of stunned relief, perhaps disbelief. I remember being surprised that a cold glass of milk was always available. I met my father and mother, uncles and cousins as strangers. I opened my closet and found nothing but wire hangers. My mother had sold and given away all my clothes. She had not expected me to return. Well, neither had I. I don't remember anger. When I went to the bank to check on the pay I had sent home to allow Ellen and me to start housekeeping, I was not surprised that Mother, whose name had to be on the account because I was a teenage soldier, had spent it all. I was home. I had changed but home had not.

Within days I married the woman who wore my engagement ring and wrote me every day when I was overseas. Looking back I think Ellen, a literature major who lived an imaginary life in post–World War I Britain, was well prepared to be a fiancée who had lost her lover in battle but not prepared to be the wife of this stranger who did not match the imaginary soldier to whom she had written so many letters.

I started classes at the university where I would later teach, astonished at the innocence of those who had not been to war. I saw them at a distance as if looking through a pair of binoculars turned backwards. They were my age—and so very young. I was determined to race through classes—something my young wife could not understand—and escape the college that was necessary if I was to vault into the middle class, get back the jobs the 4-Fs had stolen while we fought. I would, by golly, live in a single-family house.

Now, half a century and more later, I am still trying to be discharged from my war. I carry my peeled banana, my pills, my juice to the year-round porch we have built on the single-family house I own mortgage free, and study the flat, pale light just before morning when we would attack or were attacked by the enemy that rose out of the early morning shadows.

I escape from memory by flicking on the TV. There I see tanks and soldiers in the old familiar crouch my body remembers, moving against an enemy they cannot yet see. I do not know if I am watching the morning news or a documentary of an earlier war. No matter. Each year that I am further from my war, I remember more.

I have only one war buddy I see regularly; Jim Mortensen, a sergeant for whom I served as jeep driver occasionally in Berlin. But each year I am away from combat, the war grows closer. If I choose a seat in a restaurant, my back will be to the wall and I'll have a view of the door. Sitting on a friend's porch having a drink, I let part of my mind scan the lawn running down to the lake as if a field of fire. I know where I would set up my machine gun, know where the enemy would attack. Walking city streets, I note the doorways and alleys that could hide a German soldier, the windows behind which a sniper might be waiting. I look at the church steeple and scan the openings from which a rifle might suddenly appear. I find my feet making sure to be quiet, and on a walk in the woods with everyone laughing happily I am aware of land mines. Sometimes I realize my body is on patrol, alert to possible ambush.

I begin to understand how much the war marked

me, how I have made it one of my most important
identities, how I will never resolve the contradictions of
pride and shame I will always feel. And now, more than
half a century since my war, I am beginning to understand my own content in the surrealism of war and its
arctic loneliness.

One day, years ago, I wrote in my daybook, "I had an
ordinary war," and I did. But that phrase seemed to
turn a key in my memory and unlock what I thought I
had put away. In training it became ordinary to crawl
toward machine gun fire. The closer the better, because the barrel rises with its firing. It became ordinary,
after one of our colonels accidentally ordered his regiment to attack another American regiment, to drive a
jeep over the bodies of men I knew, killed by Americans, to get to the colonel's headquarters. He was removed from that command, and sent to England where,
we heard, he was promoted to general but kept far from
the command of men in battle.

The stories we tell, like the war movies—*A Midnight
Clear* or *Saving Private Ryan*—imply a buddy war, young
comrades marching toward death together, but my infantry war was one of aloneness. Looking back, I realized my strange, lonely childhood prepared me for the
surreal confusion of battle.

In combat, infantrymen keep yards from each other
so that one artillery shell, one strafing plane, one

grenade, one mortar shell will take only one soldier. In the swirl of combat, I was almost always serving with strangers. We came and went on special assignment.

I was a military policeman and often a messenger and was not surprised that I liked the lonely mission, assigned to deliver or retrieve a message, allowed to find my own way down roads without names, streets that were on no map, towns that had been reduced to rubble, fields and woods made strange by attack and counterattack.

The shame we may feel at our killing—at our being able to kill—is all retrospective. There's no time for philosophy when other human beings are trying to kill you. I don't know if I killed another person. My killing moments were all confusion. Was it my weapon, my hand grenade or someone else's that made a German tumble from a church steeple, scream from behind the wall over which I had tossed a grenade, stagger and stumble into sleep? I will never know, but I know I am brother to all who kill. I cannot stand apart from this shame.

I must also confess the fantasies that come suddenly and are played in the mind of an apparently kind elderly gent with a beard and a belly that precede him into the room. Yet in my mind, I am the one who captures the gunman who bursts into the restaurant and starts to fire. I know how I would chase the robbers as they made their escape from the bank.

Sometimes they have been more than fantasies. When Minnie Mae was carrying our first daughter, we saw a man cash a large check at a grocery store in Massachusetts then leave the groceries. The clerk and I knew what was going on. While he called for help I went after the check casher, tackling him on the roadside and literally sitting on him, feeling increasingly foolish, until the police came.

There is a dark side to my pride and my Walter Mitty fantasies. One summer day, years ago, we were driving back from Ogunquit Beach, my wife beside me, my three daughters in the back of the station wagon, when a New York driver in a Caddy tried once, twice, three times to force me off the road. Suddenly I blocked him off, got out, and pulled him out from behind the wheel and bent him backwards over the hood of his car. I held him with my left arm and body, was ready to chop my right forearm across his neck. I saw the terror in his eyes. In our intimate embrace, he knew and I knew I could kill him. I can still see his eyes, feel his breath. I let him go, and walking back to my car, I realized that a police officer had witnessed all this and done nothing, apparently thinking I was justified.

As we drove away, my hands shaking on the wheel, Minnie Mae looked at me with pride and my daughters cheered, "Daddy, the hero." But I was scared, Daddy the killer. I knew how easy it would have been. My arm knew how simple it would be, how quick.

War is an ultimate and terrible human experience that brings out the best and the worst in us. We reach the limits of exhilaration and terror, exhaustion and fear, live moments of intense feeling and blank numbness. We don't talk about that and we don't talk about the erections we sometimes get in battle. Survivor guilt is real. I do not forget the 6,286 men who were killed or wounded in my division, the 17th Airborne.

It was rarely skill, usually just dumb shit luck that kept us alive. A soldier whose name I do not remember and I went out to take a shit behind a barn high above a snow field in Belgium. We dropped our pants, squatting a couple of feet apart, and were chatting about the beauty of the scene when my companion disappeared. It is true that you do not hear the shell that kills or almost kills you. The German 88 had a shaped charge. It was focused. The soldier disappeared and I was covered with small fragments of bone, blood, skin, dirt, flesh, cloth, shit. No wounds, no Purple Heart, just sudden constipation and the familiar realization that I was lucky, no more, no less.

So much of this seemed normal then. You do what has to be done. Report his death. Go back on duty. No mourning, no memory, at least for decades. I come to realize there is a goodness, a strength in this that I have not appreciated until now, when I live my war and the life that followed in reflection.

Through most of my life, if I thought of my war, I

saw my ability to kill as a matter of shame, and yet, I
heard in my voice pride. I identified myself as a paratrooper, even during a poetry reading at West Point, enjoyed the respect of faculty and students who treated
me as one of them.

Winter makes my body return to duty. We fought the
Battle of the Bulge in a wonderland of snow. The Ardennes forest was neater than New Hampshire, but
otherwise I fought in the geography of home, the familiar grown strange by war, the beauty of my childhood
ominous in combat. On winter nights when I go to the
john as old men do, I look out on my woods that stretch
down to the riverfront. On the most beautiful nights
when moonlight moves the trees apart and the light
glistens from snow, I see, in the shadows, Germans advancing toward the house. And the old fear of moonlight when we would be revealed rises in me. I see the
scene with double vision, the beautiful woods scene
and the war landscape superimposed on it, both real,
both immediate.

And then I find myself, in this twice-lived life, admitting what I have known but never before named: I
feel a battle-tested strength in me, a feeling of confidence. I know I can do what I did not think I could do.
I am a survivor. No guilt now, just pride.

Just going from parked car to supermarket, my feet
are on patrol. I know on which foot the weight of my
body rests, where it will be a second ahead. I am, even

in the staggery years, aware of how I will attempt to move if anyone moves against me. I am alert, ready— perhaps even looking for trouble, for another testing.

Quite simply we learned we could do what had to be done. Trained by forced marches in some heat, by G.I. sergeants who tried to break us, by handling live ammunition, by running obstacle courses, and eventually by doing what had to be done under enemy fire, we explored our endurance and our limits, surprising ourselves that we could measure up.

But we kept quiet about it, even to ourselves. We saw better men than us break. We did not want to tempt the gods by bragging. But when my daughter was dying at twenty years old, which was far worse than anything I experienced in the war, I could call on my combat training and make myself nap on the waiting room floor. As it became clearer that we would have to remove extraordinary means, I had no doubt that I could. I had been tested by combat; I had withdrawn life support from my father and then my mother. I could give the gift of death to my daughter, and I did, drawing on the dark, cold strength I had developed during my years of combat.

Chapter 14

THE NOT-SO-GOOD OLD SCHOOL DAYS

Some of the dumbest people in town rise up at school budget meetings and romanticize the good old days when they were educated. They don't seem to realize their words undermine their case, but since they argue for spending less money to get better schools—a fiscal impossibility—they often carry the day. The country's politicians from presidential candidates to those running for the local school board talk education mostly to harken back to the good old days that weren't. I was there.

I thought I was stupid in school. I cannot remember when I could not read and did not spend part of every day reading. My curiosity took me through the children's shelves of the Wollaston branch library to the adult sections, where I was not supposed to read but did, and on to the huge main Thomas Crane Library in Quincy, Massachusetts, where I started making notes for one of the books I published a lifetime later. I was learning all the time—on the street, at work, at home and church and summer camp—but not in school.

As a professor and author, I have visited schools all across the United States and Canada, and even in Europe, and am amazed at how much better qualified the teachers of today are compared to my teachers. They keep going back to school themselves on evenings, weekends, and summers to improve their knowledge and their skills. They often pay for these courses themselves, and many spend their own money for books and other materials for their students.

I remember Miss Kelly in first grade, but not fondly. She often jammed me into the wastebasket, rump first, my feet up by my head like rabbit ears. The class laughed and I did not. In first grade the head of the music program told me to open my mouth and never sing because I was a monotone. I was not. I was never taught long division. My teachers were poorly educated school graduates who taught mostly by rote. In those not-so-good old days they were mostly the daughters who were chosen to take care of their aging parents. Female teachers were not allowed to marry, and in one of my high school civics classes, the police and a school board member actually came into class and removed a teacher. They did not wait until the end of class to take action, but removed her in midsentence. Her engagement announcement had appeared in the paper. The school board wasn't sure if she had done "it," but the clipping made it clear she intended to. Out she went and was immediately replaced by a single woman related to the school board member. In most school systems, it was against policy, written or unwritten, for a woman teacher, but not a man teacher, to be married. We had a lesson in political science that day.

In sixth grade I had the first teacher who challenged me, Mr. Hamilton, and I thought I was beginning to get it, but in June the tall, white-haired, imperious principal told me I would pass to the seventh grade at North Quincy Junior High School because he didn't want me in his school another year.

I was tall and sat in the back row, but I passed the eye test even though I was seriously nearsighted. How was I to know others didn't live in a blurred world, could actually see the writing on the blackboard—no green then—and could read the expression on the teacher's face? Then an uncle realized my condition and made sure I got spectacles. Miraculously, the world became sharp-edged.

My English teacher in high school punished me in the eleventh and twelfth grades when she found I had read ahead of the daily assignment, as I always did, usually reading the whole book the first night. My music teacher argued that Rimsky-Korsakov was a team like Gilbert and Sullivan. My art teacher made me use crosses for eyes. My guidance teacher gave me a B+ for a course in the eleventh grade I never attended. A history teacher jumped me between floors because I was a Scot and therefore on England's side. He was Irish and on Hitler's side. When I had the same chemistry and physics teacher in the last two years of high school, he never told me that a kid from my part of town could buy a slide rule. I got D's on five-question daily quizzes when I answered one or two questions with hand-scrawled arithmetic, while the kids with slide rules clicked their way to A's. When I did get a slide rule in the twelfth grade I was so far behind, I never figured it out—and there was no one at home who had ever seen such a contraption.

I accepted the documented fact that I was stupid, although now I realize I was placed in the highest levels of a thirteen-track system because of IQ tests, but no one explained that to me. My father hadn't gone to high school. My mother had gone to the equivalent of high school in Scotland and had been an honor student, but when I did badly she and my father blamed the teachers. They never were very interested in whether I did homework or not, and I did nothing to change that. I did, however, work hard outside of school and figured I could get ahead in the world. Even if I had difficulty learning, I believed that when I was grown up I could hire someone to do the schoolwork that bored me.

Looking back over the decades, it is hard to believe the way I felt then. Of course, I was learning on my own at a mad pace, gulping down half a dozen books or more every week, but I didn't think that was learning. It was too much fun.

I was part of the Quincy, Massachusetts, school system, nationally recognized as a good one. In Kentucky, Minnie Mae was valedictorian of her high school class at sixteen. Her father had a third-grade education; her mother went to fifth grade. They did not know a girl could go to college. They sent her seven-years-older brother to college at great financial sacrifice, but he did not once invite them to campus or tell his younger sister, a baker's daughter, that she could attend college. She won statewide awards for her singing, was an A student, yet not one teacher told her that a girl with her background could apply and attend college. She did not know there were such things as scholarships. Minnie Mae went to work. These were not the good old days for either of us.

Most of my teachers were bored with their subjects and with us. Classes consisted of forty-five to sixty students. In the tenth and eleventh grades I went to the office and officially dropped out before the end of each year. Nobody cared. In the twelfth grade John Devine and I skipped school every Thursday. Nobody noticed.

Looking back, I don't remember the anger or the despair I would expect. School was like home, something to escape. I didn't expect much from either, but I had a strange calm confidence that I couldn't articulate. If I could survive home and school, I would find a way to survive life. I was sustained by the stories I read in books and lived as much as possible within the narratives of imaginary lives. I realize that what my teachers said about writing—know what you want to say before you say it, always outline, use fancy words when a simple word will do, add as many clauses as possible to produce sentences that go on and on, write what you don't know and care about, always have a topic sentence, never use a fragment—was wrong, but my efforts to educate them failed.

I was a secret scholar. In the ninth grade I found my way into the open stacks at the library. I still dream of those stacks of books. A section, Dewey decimal 808 or 810, in the huge main library had a book by a Chicago newspaperman, Burton Rascoe, about writing. Near his book on the shelves were others on writing. I started a commonplace book decades before I knew that literary term, writing down quotes about writing by writers, beginning my lifelong study of how writers write.

When I was away from home and school, at camp, in the woods, on the city streets, at work, I thrived. If I didn't know what to do, I could learn. In school I expected failure and achieved it. At work—and later in the army—I expected to do whatever was demanded of me—and I did.

Ironically, my life was changed by a school. In the tenth grade I read a story in the *Boston Herald* about Tilton, a prep school and junior college in New Hampshire that had a program for young men who did badly at school and well at work. I wrote away for some information and forgot about it. Then one day at the Boston *Record American*, as I stood at a long line of urinals where men twice my age were staring off into a predictable future—these same urinals, these same jobs, this same pay—I realized that unless I got going, a job that was great at seventeen would still be mine at fifty-seven. I was scared into ambition.

The following Sunday a man from Tilton interviewed me at work. He had investigated me because of the letter I had written to Tilton years ago. Would I want to go to Tilton, take a course in the prep school to get my high school diploma, take a full load in the junior college, and work as a supervisor in a dormitory to earn half the $1,200 cost of tuition, room, and board? "Yes, I most certainly would. I have already saved more than $600."

Monday I went to take the $600 from my savings account. Since I was underage, I had to have my mother's name on the account. She had taken all my money. No surprise and I remember no anger. Just disappointment. I called the man from Tilton and explained that I couldn't pay my half, so I would have to turn down the opportunity. He said I was a big fellow and asked if I would play football. I said it was my dream to play football. I had worked after school and never been able to go out for the team. Arrangements were made. They were short of faculty to live in the dorm. I was put in charge of a floor.

At Tilton, I found a second great teacher, Mort Howell. I edited the school paper, played right tackle, ran a dorm floor, and in October the high school flunk-out led the class. I approached school as if it were a job. I knew how to do a job.

After the war, I was an honor student at the University of New Hampshire, doing three years in two, but before my February graduation the head of the English department, Dr. Sylvester Bingham, asked me to see him in his office. He sat me down and invited me to stay on and teach six courses in the spring semester for, I believe, $600. I was shocked. Not at the money but at the offer. I was humiliated. Me teach? It was an insult. I was a writer in my mind, not a teacher.

The Authority in the Sky has a sense of humor. I would not teach, but while writing editorials for the *Boston Herald* a few years later, I took some graduate courses at Boston University. While there, they had an emergency. Would I teach a course? Perhaps because of the seed planted by Dr. Bingham, I agreed this time and found, to my astonishment, that the class did not rise up in mutiny. Hey, I could do it. It certainly wasn't something I'd want to spend my life doing, but I could make it to the end of class, then to the end of the course. And it paid a buck or two.

A decade later, after nine years of freelancing in New York I got another call from Dr. Bingham. Would I think of returning to the University of New Hampshire, this time to set up a journalism program? The word *coitus* had appeared in the student newspaper and something had to be done. I was thirty-nine. Magazine freelancing wasn't giving me the time to write the books I wanted to write; I had three daughters, parents partly dependent on me financially; Minnie Mae was recovering from surgery; I had no health insurance and no retirement plan.

I drove to New Hampshire and the offer became firm. Teach four classes, twelve hours a week, thirty weeks a year and get paid $9,000 with health insurance and a retirement plan. Sounded like a good deal. I would have plenty of time to write—and the opportunity for revenge. I would not teach as my teachers taught but follow Dr. Bingham's counsel to teach what I knew as a professional.

I began a new life as a college professor. One course I taught was for prospective teachers. I did not know that no one else would teach it because of English department snobbery about methods courses. I went out

into the schools and found they were still teaching
what I had been taught—what I had to unlearn to become a published writer. My teaching was based on my
continuing experience as a published writer, backed up
by my commonplace book, which was, by then, twenty-
four thick loose-leaf notebooks packed with quotations
by writers.

I had a method of teaching modeled on my own
writing teacher at UNH, Dr. Carroll Towle, who had
since passed away but who had taught by individual
conferences. We wrote and shared our drafts in workshops and conference. But I felt intimidated by how little I knew about rhetoric, which was a term used in the
department that was unfamiliar to me. In the summer
before I began to teach, I read a stack of "rhetorics" and
felt simultaneously stupid and angered. I was a professional writer, but some of what they said I couldn't
understand, and most of what I did understand I thought
was wrong. The books' instructions, if followed, would
produce bad writing. It is one thing to write clearly—I
could do that—something else to articulate what I was
doing as a professional writer so that a beginner could
understand and make use of it.

Just before beginning to teach writing I had done a
story on an intercontinental missile system in which
engineers connected "black boxes" that they didn't fully
understand but that when connected produced an ef-
fective result. At the time, I was startled by what I'd

found. We had intercontinental missiles armed with hydrogen bombs directed by a guidance system that was not fully understood!

Once I stood back from the political implications of that, I found I had an engineering system I could apply to the study of writing. I looked at the entire process of writing—the prewriting that preceded the first draft, the draft, the rewriting that followed. I would break the system down and study it one part at a time.

I started backwards, examining rewriting first, because in those days I had plenty of evidence. These were the days before computers. I averaged three drafts of each magazine article with each one read ten times—thirty revisions in all, that were visible in a kite tail of drafts with inserts stapled, pasted, taped together all marked up, line by line. Minnie Mae would take this mess, type a clean draft, and I would have at it again—and again.

Once I felt I had a handle on how I revised—I discovered to my surprise that I did not so much correct error as develop what worked—I turned to prewriting and studied what I—and other writers—did before the first draft. Finally I attempted to probe the ultimate black box, the mysterious middle stage of the process when a draft was written.

I not only studied how I was writing and how other writers wrote, I learned from my students. There were always students who wrote better than others, and I

asked them to tell me—and their fellow students—
how they did it. I didn't focus on what didn't work,
which is, unfortunately, the normal way. What didn't
work seemed obvious to me. What I needed to know if
I was to teach my students responsibly and effectively
was what did work.

Dr. Richard Goodman, then superintendent of schools
in Milford and Hollis, New Hampshire, invited me to
work with a teacher in his system. Then he became
executive director of an organization of school super-
intendents, the New England School Development
Council, and he got me working with teachers in weekend and summer workshops. As I was teaching myself
to write, I was teaching others to write. Such chutzpah.
And the boy who rejected the idea of becoming a Baptist evangelist found himself an evangelist of what was
called "the writing process" method of teaching writing.

The job of teaching that I thought was part-time became the most demanding job I ever had, preparing
and teaching all sorts of writing classes and workshops,
talks, articles, and books on how to teach writing. Sweet
revenge for the high school flunk-out.

My experience visiting schools and working with
teachers makes me contradict those who say the old
days were good and the new days bad. I was impressed
by the dedication of the teachers I worked with. Most
of them paid their own way to workshops and summer
or afterschool courses. They bought professional books

to study and storybooks for their students with their own money. They worked hard to teach well while often under attack from parents, school boards, taxpayers, and sometimes even from their own administrators.

The teachers these days are far better educated than my teachers were, far more dedicated to teaching, far more willing to try new methods of teaching, and determined to reach out to the students ignored in the days of my youth, the students who come from disadvantaged homes, students with learning disabilities, students from different ethnic or language backgrounds, students with emotional, mental, or physical limitations.

In a lifetime I had moved from being one of the dumb kids sitting in the back row, to standing behind the teacher's desk, to teaching teachers. I have, indeed, lived an unexpected life.

Chapter 15

UNMASKING

In my seventies I have discovered I am not who I thought I was—and never have been. I have lived my life in mask and costume, being seen as one person while living another, more secretive life. In the mood for confession, I have occasionally revealed this private person to those closest to me, but I have rarely been believed. I have played my public role with too much skill. No surprise. I have fooled myself in the other direction, not believing the public person others know was real.

The process of deception, I suppose, begins early on. Men of my generation were taught to survive by hiding their true feelings. I came from the Scot-Yankee tradition of the stiff upper lip. My grandmother and mother, who dominated my home, held their emotions to themselves, quite possibly not even admitting them to themselves. I was taught to suppress tears (although my father was a great weeper), to control anger (although Father and

Mother lived a life of rage), not to doubt (although my parents questioned every minister's interpretation of God's Word), never to contradict (although we lived a life of contradiction), to be honest (while we built a skyscraper of family lies, one after another lifted into place).

I was, by and large, a good boy. I may have been motivated by fear of the strap, but I think in greater part by the desperate need for the love and approval that would never be there, and most of all by an elemental, animal sense of survival. Before my escape to the world beyond the backyard fence was the escape into myself.

I would wear the good boy's mask and behind it live the private life of imagination. My grandmother, my father, my mother, my uncle Will might suspect that my mind was not where my body was, but they could never be sure. I was free, behind the mask, to live not one but many secret lives. I could live safely there if I did not reveal myself.

We enjoy the myth that we like—and trust—people who are open, who are just what they seem, no more, no less, who are not sly, secretive, withdrawn. We also should know that the best mask is one of openness, the friendly, outgoing, honest face, the expression the confident artist forever wears.

The summer when I was eleven I knew I had passed a great divide into adulthood when I found that Wimpy

Ellis and I were assigned to the same tent at Camp Morgan. He kept snakes as pets, even sleeping with some of them. I was terrified of snakes, and yet for nine weeks—yes, nine snaky looooong weeks—I slept near his cot and never revealed my terror. I knew the cruelty of boys—practiced it myself—and I was certain that what happened to those who revealed their fear would happen to me.

All of us, I expect, live in fear of self-exposure. John Kenneth Galbraith, celebrated economist, writer, Harvard University professor, ambassador to India, once said, "I've never sat down to write that I don't think to myself: 'You'll be found out.'" It is only recently, however, that I have understood that since childhood and just beyond I developed a clear and consistent image of who I was and how I was seen by others. It was as if I had been accepted into the intelligence service and been given a secret identity that became my true self while I played a public part. This secret self-image determined how I related to the world. It became the way I saw experience and determined how I reacted to that experience.

I suspect that most people are guided by such a reality. When I first taught writing, meeting with each student in a weekly conference, I discovered that my view of a student's potential and accomplishment did not often match their own, and not in the way I had expected. I had thought they would think their work better than it was, but instead I often thought it better than they did, better, at least, in its possibilities.

My best students, who were mostly women, were usually the least confident. The most confident students were men who were often the least talented. The men were hilarious in their fake macho behavior, but I got mad at the women. They *must* know how good they were; they must be playing some coy feminine game of dishonesty. But as I got to know my students better, I realized this wasn't true. Their false modesty or false confidence was real, and so it became important for me to find out how the student valued the paper *before* I read it. Then I could read the paper and help the students adjust their visions to a professional standard.

It was easy to explain this by the way in which girls and boys are socialized—and there was a powerful truth in this that had to be dealt with. Women had been trained to deny their power and men to exaggerate theirs. But something else was going on. The more I taught—and consulted as a writing coach to newspapers—I found an almost direct relationship between lack of confidence and accomplishment: the less sure the student, the more sure the work.

This could be explained in part by the fact that the best writers had high standards—high ambitions—and the reality of the draft rarely comes close to the dream. But their opinions of their worth were extreme—and painful—in most cases. Publication and awards did not seem to diminish the discomfort, the sense of failure, the lack of self-worth many of the students and professionals felt. In some cases it led to people accepting roles in life that were far below their potential—and without the simple happiness that we imagine a lack of ambition brings. In other cases, the poor self-image led to emotional or mental breakdowns and, in a number of tragic cases, suicide.

In dealing with these attitudes in students, in the professionals I coached, and in the teachers that I supervised from time to time, I felt a profound empathy. I understood and shared many of their feelings, yet like them, I, too, could rarely convince myself that my work was good. In fact, I needed my own teachers to encourage me, the role that such friends as Chip Scanlan, Don Graves, and others played. They told me what I was telling my students, and in turn, when my friends revealed their own insecurities I told them what they had told me.

Now, in my seventies I have been forced to examine my self-image and have tried to revise it. I have always thought myself weak, and now I find I was—and am—physically and emotionally strong. I have survived the death of a child, the toughest test one can have, and gone on as husband, father, friend. I asked the doctor after heart surgery when they would do a procedure that they warned would be painful, and the doctor said, "We've already done it." I am, to my surprise, a tough old turkey. I have imagined myself lonely and unloved and found myself surrounded by caring family and friends. I believed I was a failure while I was succeeding, lazy when my colleagues saw me as obsessively—even obscenely and threateningly—productive.

I never thought I had talent, but I knew I had good work habits. I would be published because I showed up, delivering copy on deadline—or ahead of deadline. To this day, my Tuesday columns are sent to my editor at the *Boston Globe* on Monday, or even Sunday, a week ahead. But in these years of reconsideration, I confess, if not to talent, to an occasional delight in craft, the unexpectedly right word, a phrase that catches an elusive meaning in its claws, a clear running sentence, a well-packed paragraph. I allow myself the secret smile of the craftsperson at the workbench.

For most of my life I knew I was ugly. This was not a pretension, a modest pose, but a painful reality—to me. But in my office today I have a snapshot of a young man in his football uniform at Tilton—number thirty-nine—hands on hips, turning his smile to the camera. And beside it a paratrooper in England as yet untested by battle. Not too bad, not handsome but hardly ugly. And yet I knew I was ugly when those photos were snapped.

Looking back, I realize that over the decades I had developed a shadow persona based on accomplishment. I was shy, but I could accept an invitation to speak before five thousand people and rise to the challenge. I could accept and deliver a writing assignment with confidence while also being certain it was, if not a complete failure, not as good as it should have been, not as good as if someone else had done it.

I am amazed at how firmly I hold on to these beliefs of my own inadequacy. My mother could not accept herself or her appearance. She was an unhappy woman made to feel inadequate by her mother. She may well have had a mental illness. Certainly she had an emotional one, and she constantly ridiculed her only child's appearance. He was, in turn, too fat, too thin, too fat, too thin, then finally, in adulthood, too fat. He slumped, dressed funny, mumbled, was funny looking.

Perhaps another child would have shrugged off her daily comments, but I accepted them. If the City of Quincy had passed an ordinance that I could not go out except after dark, I would have understood. After all, she frequently told me that she never went out of the house except after dark when she carried me through the hot and humid summer of 1924. I have responded childishly aggressive to her criticism in my dress and appearance—these days a beard, bright suspenders, no socks, tailored by Wal-Mart and L.L. Bean.

My sense of being a failure is more complicated. It was reinforced by school, where I did fail again and again and again, finally flunking out of high school. Betrayed in my first marriage; fired as a writer at *Time* magazine; my rejected poems, articles, and book manuscripts all reinforced my belief that I was a failure. And yet, I realize that from the beginning I had a secret ego, even a confidence that I would succeed if not by talent then by work habits.

I lived by this belief: I was a person of limited talent and intelligence who would, by hard work and discipline, overcome my limitations and compete with those who were brighter and more talented than I. I still hold to that truth. I revel in its heroism and treasure its power of motivation. In "retirement" I get up at five-thirty in the morning and get to work early. I treasure my belief in my inadequacy.

I've found it isn't easy to give up my inadequacies, this image of myself that was constructed when I was young and by which I have lived my life. I've grown comfortable with my peculiar perception of myself. It both gives me an excuse for my failures and provides a strong negative motivation to keep me trying again and again to change that image I, ironically, hold dear.

I have had the constant love of Minnie Mae, the affection and respect of my daughters, their husbands, their children, the support of friends and colleagues, the expert counsel of a kind and wise psychiatrist, Dr. Mary Wilson, to reassure me that I have done okay—better, in fact, than might have been expected.

When I was dying during my heart attack a dozen years ago, I experienced an unexpected calm. I wanted to live, but then I checked out the insurance. I was not my father. Minnie Mae would be taken care of and so would my children. I followed the counsel of the hymn of my childhood, "to count my blessings, one by one." I did, counting as if for the first time what I had written, not what I had not written, and after having lived a life of dissatisfaction, I felt satisfaction. I had done a good job.

But having survived with the help of a triple bypass, the old feelings returned. I sit on the porch watching the light before morning sun make lacery of the winter trees and feel two contradictory emotions: pride in what I have done and the companion guilt that I have not done enough. I decide it is all right to sip a bit of pride, to feel good for the moment about myself, but then I welcome the need to do more, to strive, to work, to go downstairs to my writing desk, welcoming the familiar hunger for achievement that still drives my days.

Chapter 16

FATHERHOOD

I never wanted to have children. I write those words with shock, since I have been a father and grandfather so much of my life and only now discover as I write this that I have felt more competent, confident, and content as a father than I have been in any of the many other roles I have played: son, lover, husband, friend, soldier, student, journalist, teacher, writer. It is not that I have been a perfect father, that I haven't felt frustration, anger, pain—giving the gift of death to my daughter, twenty-year-old Lee—but that I realize I have felt less inadequacy and less doubt as a father. I have lived by the rule of love: knowing that the love was true, even if what I said or did—or did not say or did not do—was at that particular moment foolish, a mistake, or just plain wrong, it was all right. It was done—or not done—with love.

Yet for the first twenty-nine years of my life I never imagined myself a father. In fact, I knew for certain I would never be one. There have been moments

when my parents felt joy, love, satisfaction, complete-
ness in me, but I was not aware of a single time. I was a
responsibility to them, a duty, an obligation, a burden,
and although I eventually became a financial resource,
what I provided was never enough. I told myself I
would not take on the burden of having a child. Never.
There seemed no benefits, no joy, no satisfactions, just
another burden, another duty without reward.

I was always amazed at the alien world of my play-
mates who had families that could absorb me, where
Father was proud to be a father and took delight in his
children, where Mother was motherly, affectionate,
caring, joyful in her family. Not so at my home and not
in my cousins' homes. There was instead a sense of obligation and a worshipful admiration for the widowed
mothers of my father and mother who each raised a
family on their own in a foreign land. My parents had a
duty to care for their mothers but no affection or apparent delight in their companionship.

My uncle Don, for whom I had been named, was
a bachelor and seemingly the happiest of my uncles. I
just assumed I would lead his single life. But there
was a problem. I was obsessed with sex. The more my
mother made it clear that love, courtship, romance,
and sex were evil, devices the woman devil used to cor-
rupt men, the more I sought corruption. It was the era
of the sweater girl, and I spent most of my waking and
most of my sleeping hours imagining what was under

those sweaters, especially the angora ones that rose and fell with such furry delight. I found out later—far later—what was hidden under the sweaters: contraptions. And even what was under the contraptions, but the end of mystery did not seem to decrease desire.

The army sent me to the University of New Hampshire for four weeks and I met a coed who had been a neighbor when I was in kindergarten. She and I both were galloping away from strange and unhappy family lives, but of course, we thought it was love. Wartime was a time of romance. We were told it in short stories and novels, in movies and stage plays, in song and observation. Before I was sent overseas we were engaged, and she wrote me daily. When I came home from the war we were married in days and became one of the first couples allowed to break the rule at the University of New Hampshire that undergraduates could not be married. It would be immoral. We might contaminate the innocent single and virginal students. Before the ceremony witnessed by her mother and aunt, my father and mother, and the dust covers on the furniture of the parsonage—the minister had just returned from being a navy chaplain—we both agreed we would never, ever have children.

If we had lived together before marriage, as our successfully married daughters did, I think we would have broken up by spring vacation, but we didn't, not in those days. I thought I was happily married for life, that

love had given me what my parents did not have, until
one day someone told me—I can still stand in that spot
in Murkland Hall at the University of New Hampshire
and feel the emanations of surprise—what I must have
already known: there was someone else in my wife's
life. Fortunately we had no children, and after my escape through divorce, the first in a family with genera-
tions of unhappy marriages, I promised myself I would
never marry again and therefore I would never have
children.

I became a copyboy in Boston, then a reporter, lived
in a rooming house on Commonwealth Avenue and
then in a couple of one-room apartments on the back
side of fashionable Beacon Hill. I liked living alone
with my books, my phonograph records, the novels and
poems I wrote, then burned in moments of glorious
self-pity and satisfying despair.

Then Minnie Mae Emmerich appeared. She was a
substitute blind date one night in 1951. I asked her out
to dinner but she said she'd cook in. Before I knew it
we had a fourth date and a fifth. She made it clear she
was not prepared to even think of marriage, and that
was a great relief to me. But eleven months later, before the year was out, with no proposal either of us can
remember, we were married.

I don't remember any mention of children before or
after the ceremony. I certainly didn't bring the subject
up. I saw myself turn from lover into husband but

could not imagine myself a father, assuming I'd be a
failure at the job, and therefore it wouldn't be fair to
the kids I didn't want to have anyway.

There are marriages that are built and rebuilt on
long serious talks. Not ours. Minnie Mae has said, "A
good talk could destroy a marriage." So one day Minnie
Mae, who is five years older than I am, said, without
any warning, "I guess if we're going to have children,
it's time." I wish I could remember joy, terror, wonder, apprehension, celebration, anger, betrayal, antici-
pation, something. But I'm afraid that I reacted as if
she had just said she was going to take up horseback
riding, repaint the bedroom, plant zinnias in her garden. "Well, if you want to," I said. This was fine with
Minnie Mae. She didn't want talk but action.

As things developed I remember some financial concerns, but Minnie Mae said she would go back to work
(which she didn't) and I told myself that when the baby
came I'd react instinctively—an amazingly wise decision in retrospect.

Events became exciting toward the end of her first
pregnancy. Minnie Mae sang "Jubilate Deo" as mezzo-
soprano soloist at Emmanuel Church in Boston and
then a few days later called me to say that a checkup
showed she might be suffering toxemia, also called
eclampsia—the primary reason, we were told, for having the prenatal care our mothers did not have. In Minnie Mae fashion she drove in from Wellesley to pick

me up at the office and then drove us to Beth Israel Hospital.

The news was not good. I was told that mother and baby had a fifty-fifty chance of survival and that if the baby lived, the chances were about 100 percent it would be blind. I was asked if I wanted to see a Dr. Green who could tell me the best way to tell my wife the news if the baby was blind. I saw him. There is no good way.

Things were different in 1953. Care at Beth Israel, one of the top hospitals in the country, meant I was not even allowed on the same floor during Minnie Mae's thirty-hour labor. I waited in the main lobby until Dr. Louis Zetzel, a wonderful doctor and sensitive man by the standards of the day, walked over to me, rapped the back of his hand against my fly, and said, "Keep it zipped up." Then, and only then, did he tell me that mother and child were fine, but that we were to have no more children.

Minnie Mae, sick from anesthesia, was not allowed to see our daughter, Anne, who was born premature, but I could see her through the nursery window, which was decorated with a Christmas scene and a six-pointed star that brought tears to my eyes. Still does. I was not allowed to hold Anne—and Minnie Mae would not see her for two days although Anne's weight was normal—but I knew I was a father. It was instantaneous. Instinct had clicked in. I felt relief, joy, and a surprising confidence. Love would instruct.

And it did. I don't remember holding a single baby before I first held Anne, but it was as natural as if I'd been a father for years. The bond was immediate, the circle of family complete. And when we moved to New York—just after I had said I would never move to New York—Minnie Mae went to Dr. Saul Gusberg at Columbia-Presbyterian, who in turn sent her to Dr. Tilman, who had studied Catholic and Orthodox Jewish women who had toxemia and ignored the medical advice never to have more children. They had more children, but had no more toxemia.

With my enthusiastic support this time, we decided to have another baby but no luck. Minnie Mae's mother, at my invitation, had moved in with us. A wise family doctor, Marty Gold, said, "Go away for a weekend," and so we had a second daughter, Lee. No toxemia. And then a third, Hannah, without toxemia. We would not have stopped except for Minnie Mae's age, thirty-nine, then considered late for having children.

Each daughter was different, a wonderful, amazing, and ever developing combination of mother and father and, best of all, themselves. Of course, we must have had problems, conflicts, anger, frustrations, fears, but mostly I remember the joys, the small sentimental ones—the tiny hand in mine, the baby snuggled into my shoulder, Anne's first-child seriousness, Lee's healing joy, Hannah's wisdom, each individual girl's sense of humor. I was lucky. When my children were young I

was freelancing. There was a continual terror to that—
one year we went eleven months without income, one
Christmas we bought all the holiday food and presents
after a check arrived at 11 A.M. on Christmas Eve—but
I was home with my children unlike most fathers of the
time. At thirty-nine, I became a professor with a regular
check in the mail, but I lived less than a mile from my
office and continued to share the daily companionship
of Minnie Mae, Anne, Lee, and Hannah.

One evening in 1977 I received a phone call from
Paul Escholz asking me to teach in a summer program
at the University of Vermont. I said, "No, thanks." And
then the phone rang again. Our middle daughter, Lee,
now a sophomore at the University of Massachusetts,
had just been accepted as an oboe student by the New
England Conservatory of Music. She asked if we could
afford the increased tuition. We could. It was the exact
dollar amount I had been offered to teach in the summer program at Vermont. I called back, "Yes."

And then, before the program was over in August,
we received a phone call from our other daughters. Lee
was terribly sick and was being taken to Exeter Hospital by ambulance. Because of an unusual diagnosis by
Dr. James Tucker, Lee was then rushed by ambulance
to Massachusetts General Hospital in Boston. She suffered from Reye's syndrome, a terrible disease we had
never heard of that may be the result of taking aspirin
during a viral illness and is wrongly thought to attack

only children between the ages of three and twelve. It rages throughout the system, attacking many organs, especially the liver and the brain.

We were able to speak to her at Exeter Hospital just before the ambulance took her to Boston, and she told us how wonderfully her sisters had taken care of her when she had a fever and was sick to her stomach. By the time she arrived in Boston, Lee was unconscious.

Minnie Mae, Anne, Hannah, and Lee's boyfriend, Paul Lambert, stood vigil in a tiny waiting room that served a huge intensive-care facility. For four and a half days we were crowded only once. Experts from around the country, Europe, and the U.S. Center for Disease Control in Atlanta were called. Eighty percent of those who have Reye's syndrome pass a crisis and leave the hospital as healthy as they were before it struck. We were, in a sense, back in the medical era of my childhood waiting for the crisis to pass. I do not know where her mother, her sisters, her boyfriend got their strength. I know where I got mine: from my love of them and from my survival in battle when I discovered I could do what I did not think I—or any man—could do. I was even able to lie on the cold floor of that waiting room and sleep as I had under shellfire, knowing I had to preserve my strength to do my job as a father.

The crisis did not pass. We each visited with her alone and executed the decision to withdraw extraordinary means.

I had made the decision to give the gift of death to my father when he was seventy-nine, to my mother at eighty-two, and now to my sunny, happy middle child at twenty. I was given a social worker's office, and she asked if there was anything she could do. I snapped, "Get the hell out." Later she refused my apology. She understood. Before they pulled the plug on the respirator, I called the funeral home. I still dream that Lee rises up laughing at the other end of the corridor, telling us it was all a joke. It was not. It was the loneliest moment of my life.

"How can you go on?" people have asked.

Losing a child is the worst thing that I have ever experienced, and yet, even in that horrible moment, I was glad to be a father, to have known Lee, to be able to give her what she needed at that moment, even if it was death.

Years later I wrote a poem that contains my frustration and rage.

> LEE
> *Remember me not*
> *when I was kept from you*
> *in the waiting room, not*
> *when I sat in an office signing*
> *your dying, not*
> *when I pushed you on the swing*
> *higher than you had ever flown*

and you looked back as I grew small,
certain I would always be able
to save you.

But there was no time for rage. I was not alone. I had Minnie Mae, Anne, Hannah, and Lee's boyfriend, Paul. There was no choice. I could not run away. I could not suffer a nervous breakdown as my father had at business deaths. I could not get drunk as I had done so well when I was younger. No. No. I was husband and father. I would do what Lee would have wanted me to do.

I did learn that day that we have the right to grieve in our own way. I will never forget when we came home and I fell into the green chair in the living room, feeling I would never move again. The next thing I knew, the Heilbronners brought food and Phyllis was on her knees next to the chair feeding me.

The night of the day Lee died we went to a performance of *The Sound of Music.* Hannah was in the chorus. Life must go on. We sleepwalked through those days. We had no formal funeral. We had no strength for that after the week in the hospital. We had the cremation that we discovered from Paul was Lee's preference, expressed after a college friend of theirs had died in an automobile accident. We had a graveside service at the Durham cemetery with Don Graves, one of my closest friends, a writer and professor who is ordained, and Father Joseph Desmond, since Paul was Catholic. Paul attended with his parents, and there were Anne, Hannah, Minnie Mae, and myself.

When we returned to the house after the service there was more food from our neighbors. Later we learned that the Heilbronners, the Lindens, the Clarks, the Graveses, the Ladds, the Robinsons, the Bradley-Swifts, and others kept an eye out and made sure we had support—and privacy.

There is no one way to grieve. Minnie Mae did not cry. I poured like the Niagara Falls. She did not grieve less and I did not grieve more. I felt as if I were walking in an ocean of molasses, each step slow and difficult. It was August and the university offered me the semester off. I refused. I needed habit, ritual, purpose, work. In each class I told a student I trusted what had gone on so they could cancel the class if I broke down.

After class I'd have no memory of what I'd taught or how, what students had said in the discussion and what I'd said in response, but I'd check with the student whom I'd told and found I'd done my job.

I learned many things from Lee's death. I had been writing a letter of condolence, thinking it was probably a waste of time, when we received the first call from her sisters that Lee was sick. I discovered it was better to say something than to say nothing. A few days after Lee's death I was in the supermarket and a colleague was pushing his wife in a wheelchair. She had brain damage. Before Lee's death, I probably would have avoided them and escaped up the next aisle. I found myself going to them, touching and speaking. I knew how important it was to reach out, to touch, to make eye contact, to speak of the unspeakable.

One of my neighbors who had lost a son himself gave me a strange and significant comfort: "It will never get any better." I was surprised and puzzled by his remark, but in the days ahead I learned what he meant. Lee's death had become part of me. It was what I was. I would feel it always. And most of all, I would never forget Lee. How terrible it would be to forget her standing outside Hannah's playpen, making her laugh; not hearing her practice Albinoni from the next room; forgetting her passion for submarine sandwiches; putting out of mind the time I sat in the middle of the orchestra with her and the long talk we had afterwards on the ride home from Amherst. And I would not want to forget her standing at the end of that long tunnel waiting during my heart attack or all the times she has visited us since, standing in the shadows at the edge of the door, suddenly appearing at my side as I write, talking to me, making me laugh. No. I do not forget and I am glad of it, tears or not.

I am glad I was so wrong when I did not want children. I am grateful to be Lee's father still, to be part of the family Minnie Mae and I have constructed from our love and that will continue after we have gone, to have watched Anne and Hannah grow into mature women, to become father-in-law to Michael and Karl, grandfather to Joshua, Samuel, and Michaela.

I, who did not want to have children, cannot imagine my life if I had not become a father.

Chapter 17

TAKING CARE

I was deep asleep, far beyond the world of dreams, when Minnie Mae hit me and made animal sounds. As I jumped out of bed and turned on the light I looked at the clock: twelve thirty-five in the morning. She was outside the covers lying crosswise on our king-size bed grunting, her arms and legs flailing. I grabbed her hands and pulled her up into the sitting position she assumes when she wakes me with the low blood sugar of a diabetic.

I asked her if it was blood sugar. She couldn't talk and she wasn't sweaty as she usually is and her pulse didn't seem to be racing as it does when she needs orange juice in a hurry. I heard none of the slurring associated with a stroke and both sides of her body seemed equally agitated. I stupidly kept asking her if she wanted me to call the doctor, call 911, take her to the hospital. She nodded no each time, and it was clear she was in no condition to make a decision. It was my decision alone.

In that moment, I went back to where I had been in combat. Cold. Calm. Efficient. The world slowed down by adrenaline, and I had that strange combat confidence that I could do what had to be done, face what had to be faced. I was detached from my anxious, terrified self. Later Minnie Mae told me she knew I would be that way, scared and worried about her but cold and efficient, ready to do what had to be done. It was how I had felt about her when I went into heart surgery.

We have an old-fashioned doctor whose home number is in the phone book. I woke him and he told me to call 911. The dispatcher kept me on the line, allowing me only to open the garage door and put on the outside lights. Minnie Mae had slumped back across the bed and could no longer respond to me by nodding. Her convulsions increased in the minutes before members of the Durham Fire Department and Ambulance Corps crowded into the room. I had a combat flashback—quicker, more complete, in bright black and white as if the scene were lighted by flares—of soldiers dying in exactly the same way Minnie Mae was behaving, and I was running past them as I would have had to in an attack. I thought I had lost her.

The EMT in charge asked me about her, and I said that she had diabetes, Parkinson's, and did not have heart trouble. I handed him the plastic-covered list of our medications I always have with me. He took her blood sugar—13—while others tried to rouse her and couldn't. He jammed a packet of sugar in her mouth that she was unable to swallow and later spat out, and then he gave her a shot and started an IV. Others took her blood pressure and monitored her heart.

We kept trying to get her to respond until, at last, she seemed to give me a smile of recognition. Later she told me she realized that people were working on somebody and then realized the somebody was her. They took her blood sugar: 203. Minnie Mae would make it. Still unconscious, she was put on a stretcher and taken to the hospital.

I followed the ambulance to the hospital, where Minnie Mae gained consciousness as they treated and examined her, allowing me to be at her side as she dozed and woke and dozed again. Her blood sugar went down to 110, then 70. Her EKG, blood, and urine tests were good, as well. At four in the morning she was discharged with orders to get something sweet on the way home.

At four-thirty, just four hours after she woke me, we were at an all-night Dunkin' Donuts eating doughnuts and drinking orange juice—I decided I deserved a couple, as well. At five-thirty she was back in her bed asleep and I was awake—wide awake—for the next seventeen hours telling the story of the night in my head, on the phone with my daughters and friends, and on paper, writing to record, study, and understand as is my habit—and my responsibility as her caretaker as she is mine.

We don't know what caused the unexpectedly low blood sugar. She had started on a new diabetic medication weeks before, and Minnie Mae, under doctor's orders, had lowered her insulin. After this incident it was lowered again. She thought she had eaten enough. I didn't but then she always does and I always disagree. She hadn't taken a diabetic snack as she hadn't for years but is now.

I wonder if I should have forced her to eat more, but that issue is at the center of our ever changing relationship as we age. One moment I am her caretaker, another her partner, still another her husband, her friend, her lover; the roles extend and interact.

Recently Minnie Mae's Parkinson's medication had to be doubled with the warning it might cause some confusion. It has but not in any way I expected. We have to learn together. For all the years of our marriage she has kept the financial accounts. Now it is extremely difficult, and we have hired a bookkeeper from our accountant's office.

Minnie Mae's confusion is slight and usually matches mine. What is so-and-so's name? What day is it? What are we doing today? But then there are surprises. Minnie Mae has been giving herself insulin injections for at least fifteen years. Then one day she said she didn't know how. I had to teach her. Now she's on oral medication but I have to monitor her taking it. The other morning she told me she had decided not to take her prescriptions anymore. I am amazed. I am calm. I ask if she wants to call the doctor or should I? She tells me to. I talk to Tracy, Dr. Olney's nurse, and Minnie Mae agrees to take her pills.

These days, when our daughters visit, I hear the tone they use with their children and then I hear the same voice I use with Minnie Mae. I am horrified, yet she is not upset. This additional Parkinson's medication seems to have eliminated most of her "affect." She is not emotionally upset, hurt, or defensive if I have to correct or direct her as I would a child.

I am amazed at my patience—so is Minnie Mae— during these years that we have been living with Parkinson's. It is the last quality I ever expected to discover in myself. I am delighted and astonished, as surprised as our children and our friends. But how can you be impatient with someone whose brain has made the world move slowly? Minnie Mae may slip a cog once in a while, as I do, but she has her sense of humor, her intelligence, and we have, if anything, a sweeter, kinder relationship while we care for each other.

It is a two-way street. When I come home in the early morning from having coffee with my cronies at the Bagelry and the upstairs is quiet, I often creep upstairs on the outside of the steps so they will not betray me, and stand by our bed waiting to see if the sheets move and my wife still breathes, the way I waited as a boy by Grandma's bed.

This morning she wakes and smiles. She knows my habit, and I wave and go back downstairs to my writing desk. Old, we have become watchers for what we only too well know.

"Anything wrong?" Minnie Mae asks as we sit in a companionable silence reading.

"No," I grump. "Why?"

"You made a funny noise."

"Didn't."

"Did."

"Just breathing. That all right?"

"Good idea, breathing."

Waking in the night, I listen for the sounds of Minnie Mae sleeping and know, when she wakes, she listens for me. We watch each other out of the corners of our eyes, reading the tint of skin, the hesitant step, the tremor in the hand, the time it takes for a word to travel from thought to speech, the time it takes for the fork to find the mouth.

We are alert for inflection, pause, pace, grimace, groan, deep breath, sigh, gasp, hearing what is not said, watching what is not done. Married forty-nine years, we are familiar with each other's commonplace habits and keep reading new meaning into old behaviors. It is wise. It is what we must do, to make sure the other person is on the right side of denial or concern.

Coming from a generation of ignoring complaints and toughing it out, we now accept this alertness that must probe each other's privacy. One Sunday afternoon Minnie Mae started to hemorrhage, and ever since I worry something like this may happen again; I have had my heart attack and will not be surprised at another. We must take account of symptoms and dismiss most of them; denial, after all, is dangerous but necessary if we are to carry on, but we must try to make sure that the other person's ignoring is correct.

Being watched is sometimes touching, mostly irritating. My answers to Minnie Mae's inquiries are usually grouchy. Why? Because the twinge in the chest, the unexpected feeling of pressure, the "indigestion," the sudden lightheaded vertigo, the stagger, the lost noun are all frightening, and we are trying to brush aside the fear, not confident that it is the right decision when a concerned wife brings worry back to the surface. Of course, I grump. Of course, I am guilty of grumping. Of course, I am hurt when she grumps at my concerned question.

Our concern for the other is rooted in fear, more for the loss of the other than for ourselves. And the complex feelings behind the simple questions we ask each other lie deep within us.

My father undercut my childhood by making me his confidant and more—his spy. I can remember in houses or apartments in which we lived before I went to first grade, my father asking me, "Is Mother all right?" "Does Mother seem changed?" "Do you think Mother is worse?" All my life he asked these questions, teaching me to look at Mother as a clinical psychologist assessing her emotional and mental health. He may have had good reason, and of course, Mother, and Grandma, and Uncle Will, and Uncle Don, and Uncle Alec were all critical of my father, making me study him to see if I saw their signs of weakness: a certain deaconish, customer-is-always-right obsequious unmanliness, and the always dreaded nervous breakdown when he took to bed after a business decision gone bad or when he was "let go."

We have been told about children who were encouraged in Nazi Germany, Communist Russia or China, to take account of their parents' political health and report them if necessary, but I wonder how many parents today, especially in an age of divorce, single parents, and boyfriends or girlfriends who sleep over, make confidants of their children, involving them in domestic spy networks.

Of course, as a kid, I loved each betrayal—and thought as Father gossiped about Mother and Mother gossiped about Father that I would begin to understand the mysteries of my family. Of course, I did not. Each revelation peeled away revealed a deeper mystery, an old hurt, fear, hate, worry, wound.

Now I draw Hannah or Anne aside. "How do you think Mother's doing? Have you noticed any changes since—" And I stop. I hear my father's words come from my mouth. And I feel the uncomfortable invitation to betrayal. They look at me and understand. We stumble forward, speaking in half sentences, each holding back a bit.

And yet it is right that I should ask them, even a few close friends, because I am too familiar to notice changes or there are changes I might accept because each daily increment is so small. So I open the door to their spying, their invasion of Minnie Mae's privacy, and imagine that she is doing the same about me.

I remember my irritation when my parents did not get the medical help they needed, when they ignored symptoms, or were loyal to doctors I thought old and out of touch, when they resisted another test, another diagnosis. Now I find Minnie Mae—and myself—delaying. She needs yet another operation on a drooping eyelid that hampers her vision. Her delay irritates me. It is a simple operation. But I no longer heckle. It is her eye. "There is only so much . . ." she says. I understand. We are to schedule a sigmoidoscopy. We will—as soon as we can face it. Let's get over that low blood sugar incident first. And those operations for my trigger fingers? Later.

Minnie Mae was taking action to deal with her painful, bent-over back, when a routine mammogram brought a new challenge. We have strength for only one disease at a time. She was heroic about the breast cancer, but the back and the eye went to the back burner. Now the back is being dealt with, and the eye and who knows what else will be on the front burner soon.

We have dinner with Marcy Carsey, a television producer and former student. Marcy is wonderful and draws Minnie Mae out, getting her to talk about her years in the Pentagon, the scientists who worked out of the office where she was secretary, her Q clearance, her global view of the war.

I sit back, impressed at the respect and interest that Marcy expresses for this woman she has just met, and I am amazed at how much my wife, a modest and retiring woman in such situations, is saying. I feel one of those always unexpected, always overwhelming gasps of love for this woman who has experienced and survived so much and always kept her sense of humor on a hair trigger. And at the same time I am her caretaker as well as her lover, and I take clinical account of the slowness of her speech. She says more than usual because Marcy is such a good audience, and I am aware that I have a chance to observe her speech, the river of words I hardly ever hear because we speak in quick shorthand. And so I study the flow of words, feeling both my distance, my betrayal, my respect, and my love.

It seems to me that the flow is a bit slower. Minnie Mae hesitates and asks me for a name or a place, as we do so often, and Marcy, with enormous understanding and kindness, brings the unspoken out in the open, asking Minnie Mae what it is like to have Parkinson's, what the difficulties are in getting the words from brain to tongue. We already know that Marcy's husband has suffered strokes, so we're sure she understands. Later we note how kind and perceptive that was, how much better it is to have things out in the open, not ignored, passed over as if they didn't exist.

But, even as a writer who always has part of his mind at a distance, observing, taking note, and who has accepted this as part of his nature to always have a certain detachment even in the most involved moments, I feel I should not be evaluating Minnie Mae's speech. But I should. I need to be alert to what I can do and not do.

Parkinson's affects Minnie Mae's balance and her gait; her eye surgeries affect her depth perception; osteoporosis and Parkinson's afflict her back. I must be aware if she needs my help—and I must accord her independence and respect. Years ago, in doing research for a story on the doubly afflicted "deafblind," I discovered that parents of blind children are usually far more patient and less abusive than parents of deaf children. Why? With a blind child the parent is in control. It is the child who has failings. With a deaf child it is the parent who has failed to communicate, and failure leads to frustration and, often, anger. I need to help Minnie Mae but never take away her independence, her ability to control.

We have become very good at a secret dance, my hand near if she needs it. When I give her my hand as she gets out of a chair, I do not yank. I just hold the hand steady. She pulls herself up. She is in control. She wants to get in and out of the car. I let her. To hell with public courtesy. She wants to push the heaping grocery cart, go ahead. But I must be aware of the curb, the stairs, the step down—or up—into the next room at the restaurant. And if I don't know if she wants help, I ask. It is her decision, not mine. I have a fear of being the aggressively thoughtful, caring, loving husband, drawing attention to my public virtue.

Of course, there is another distance we must keep. We are the medical corps people, the medical reporter who is on the scene. We have taken to sitting in on most of each other's physical examinations so we can help remember the answers to our doctors' questions— how long, when were you, what was the diagnosis, how much did you take, how often. The observer patient corrects not only fact but nuance, adjusting our need for denial and placing "incidents" in context. Our doctors seem to accept, even appreciate, our team approach.

I was glad to be part of all the discussions about

treatments with Minnie Mae's oncologist, surgeon, and radiation physician, but what fascinated and impressed me was the fact that in every case when Minnie Mae had to make a treatment decision—whether on a core biopsy, yes, versus a needle biopsy, no; a mastectomy, no, versus a lumpectomy, yes; radiation, yes, and chemotherapy, no—her usually slow reactions and speech were quick and positive.

I must watch Minnie Mae as she must watch me. But my watching, as hers must, as well, leads to another betrayal. We have to prepare for the future by imagining it. I have always lived multiple imagined lives, making believe I really would "die before I wake," would somehow live forever in the furnace flames of hell, would get St. Vitus' dance or locomotor ataxia like the man down the street who had syphilis, or have my face frozen into a grimace or get blood poisoning from a rusty nail as Uncle Alec did and have a stiff finger, or drown as I almost did three times.

At the other end of life, after we found that the secret imaginings about the death of a child could come true, I find my mind is full of imaginings, not so much about myself, although there are some, but about Minnie Mae. It is clear she can no longer live alone. She depends on me. I am glad to be here and hope I will be as long as I can help. I imagine she has fallen, she has some new disease or an old one has advanced; I care for her at home or visit her in the nursing home, perhaps sharing a room or wheeling down from the men's wing, or I go upstairs some morning and the covers do not move.

I live here alone or marry again or live near a child or in a child's home, the old man in the upstairs bedroom, or in a nursing home. Each imagining is a betrayal or, perhaps, I try to tell myself, a necessary preparation, a rehearsal for what I may have to endure or, dying, leave.

I watch our own increasing frailty, our losing control, our dying and then turn my mind off, usually by getting up and doing something, anything that brings me back to the present—robbing the icebox, going to the can, catching my face in the mirror and seeing a look I could never read on my father's face, an ironic half smile as if he could not quite believe what he was imagining. Perhaps he had been watching what he did not want to see and, for the moment, could not look away.

In these late years of our lives we watch the past and the present and the future. Minnie Mae takes a long time in the ladies' room, disappears down a supermarket aisle, does not hear me when I call from the other room, and the imaginings begin. She worries before I go down to Boston to have breakfast with Chip, who is working there for a week, concerned I will fall asleep at the wheel, that the weather will be bad, that road construction . . . and I get irritated, feeling the leash tight about my neck. For this reason we have a cellular phone. I call her when I leave and along the way. Not just as a matter of concern but because I worry she may have fallen, something may have happened. When she does not answer, the mind movies begin and I call again. She answers. We look out for each other, twined by love and habit and the years of caring that we hope will go on forever and that we know cannot.

Chapter 18

COMRADES

We live in New England, where people are friendly but keep their distance. Age closes that distance, at least for me. After we lost our daughter I found the worst thing was avoidance, a turning away, silence. It is true that people do not know what to say, but saying nothing is worse than saying something wrong. Ever since then, I do not avoid. When the young politely look away from the old lady with the three-pronged cane, the man in the wheelchair, the woman with the walker in the doctor's waiting room, the radiation center, at the drug store, in the restaurant, I look them in the eye and speak. We are comrades in the battle to survive. The response is usually surprise, followed by pleasure. They are suddenly individuals again, not a category. We share a wry smile, an ironic look, sometimes a touch, usually a line or two of black humor: "Oh, to be seventy again."

These momentary encounters remind me of the wartime conversations I had with my comrades on a troop train, shipboard, or in a foxhole. We shared a companionship of common terror with a black humor, and I often find myself today trying a similar tactic with comrades heading toward the battles of aging: "I'm in good shape for the shape I'm in."

As in combat, a deep if passing comradeship can develop in the face of reality, and sometimes we are able to serve together during a long campaign. Art and Barbara Robinson were living diagonally across the street when we built our house in 1963. They had no children and enjoyed ours; we had no dog and enjoyed theirs. They also shared our tears at the loss of Lee and celebrated with us the weddings of her sisters. We were Yankee neighbors, stopping to talk about the Red Sox, the university's latest ridiculousness, town gossip. We never visited for long. We perched on their living room couch—not taking off our coats—and less often, they visited in our house and we occasionally ate together. When they went away—rarely—and when we went away—frequently—we checked on each other's houses. Then one night the phone rang while I was asleep.

"It's Art," said Barbara.

"I'll be right there," I answered, tugging on my clothes and seeing the EMTs sliding Art into the ambulance. I pulled my Jeep out of the drive and drove to where Barbara was waiting. As she clambered in on one side, the fire department captain leaned in on my side and whispered in my ear, "He's gone," so I would be prepared to help Barbara at the hospital. Barbara was made of stern stuff. She handled her own affairs. But we were comrades as we faced Art's death.

Barbara's closest relative was a niece—a former student of mine—who lives in Georgia. Minnie Mae and I served as Barbara's family at the Masonic service and later at the funeral. We became family. Barbara, who loved to go out and eat as we did, went to the movies with us and would come over, at a moment's notice, to share pot luck, watch a movie on our VCR, football or hockey on television.

We kept an eye on each other, calling if we saw a light late at night when it shouldn't be on or off when it should be on. In this comradeship of the aging, we'd note how long a strange car stood in the driveway and stop by if we thought anything wrong. It was two-way duty and we each appreciated the other's nosiness. And although she would have scoffed at the idea, her courage made her a mentor, showing us how to behave if one of us was to go before the other. She instructed by behavior, no sermons, on how to handle loss and loneliness, when to be independent and when to allow others to help.

Then one February Barbara fell on the ice and couldn't get up. Another neighbor, Dr. Cindy Cooper, found her and drove Barbara to the hospital. Dr. Cooper called us and we became even closer comrades to Barbara in the next ninety-four days.

We rushed to the Wentworth-Douglass Hospital in Dover, New Hampshire, and were immediately treated as if we were family, allowed to visit her at will and given clear and careful explanations of what each test showed. The fall wasn't anything to worry about, but routine tests led to not-so-routine tests.

We became intimate companions, even at times participants in her battle, and all the time knew we were experiencing a dress rehearsal for what might happen to one or both of us. We cared for Barbara, visiting her once, twice, or three times a day, consulting with nurses and doctors, communicating with her niece, investigating treatments and care facilities, even searching her house for financial records and inventorying them. It turned out to be more time-consuming than we ever imagined but far more comforting than we had expected.

It wasn't all wonderful. It was cancer. The nurses were universally caring. We kept expecting to run into the evil nurse—there must be one—as we dropped by early in the morning, during the day, late at night. We never found her. The nurses and nurse's aides were all caring, open, and both professional and nonprofessionally friendly.

The doctors? Well, there wasn't one doctor in charge.

There were many doctors, specialists with overlapping responsibilities and irresponsibilities. They came and went—skiing, to conventions, on vacation, off on weekends. They were covered by colleagues who, in turn, were covered by other colleagues. They each had territories—was it the bladder or the uterus or what? The doctors ranged from concerned to disinterested, and what we learned was that the patient needs an aggressive advocate, hopefully a primary-care physician, but at least a tough questioning family member.

Barbara did not want her niece, a busy teacher and mother, to trek up to New Hampshire, and so decisions were made at a distance and, in some cases, by default. Barbara had a living will and it was our duty to see that it was in place at each facility, but when the doctors asked her if she wanted a procedure, it was not clear if she understood what was being asked. Most of the time she was clear, bright, informed, but other times she was sedated and confused. The doctors did as I would in an age of medical litigation, performed the procedure that would avoid a lawsuit even if it didn't do very much to improve her life. Barbara probably didn't need the surgery followed by radiation.

During Barbara's long dying, we learned that the living will and power of attorney were not so easily exercised when the patient drifted back and forth between the rational and the delusional; when questions such as "Do you want to be resuscitated?" were asked and she had a high fever, had just been moved to a new institution or room, or was being treated with drugs to battle pain or anxiety.

As we cared for Barbara, we told our children that one of them might have to become our advocate immediately. Don't be shy. Look at the medical records. Be aggressive. Most doctors are not comfortable talking about death or lives that have little quality. Their job is treatment and they are very good at that. And they believe they can get into more legal trouble for not treating than for treating.

We found out that when the doctors asked Barbara, "Do you want treatment?" she was in the worst possible physical, emotional, and mental condition to answer their questions.

She didn't arrive in the hospital because she was healthy. She had a fever, a chemical imbalance that affected her judgment. She was suffering pain and considerable confusion, not even knowing if she was in a hospital or nursing home at times. She was a tough woman but not able to absorb a prognosis that was so serious that no treatment might have been the best treatment.

We were astonished at the number of doctors who saw Barbara in the first few days, then went away for the weekend or on vacation and were replaced by associates or substitute associates. These associates were often specialists who seemed to see her as an individual organ or system, not a whole person. They openly told us they disagreed with each other, and they did not seem to be communicating with each other even if they were in the same practice.

We tried not to waste our energies on anger; that is the design of today's medical profession. But we were not family. We could not demand answers to the cost in pain and suffering of each treatment and the effect on her lifestyle after she was treated. The jokes are true: "The treatment was successful but we lost the patient"—or worse, the patient lingers on in a half—or quarter—life.

The living will Barbara drafted in a lawyer's office, as we have, was not as helpful as we expected. If we lie in a vegetative state after all sorts of treatments have failed, the living will may be invoked. But Barbara was alive and usually rational yet unable to ask the tough questions she should have asked about the quality of life she would have—if the treatment was successful.

The living will doesn't go into effect if we are of clear mind; in reality, the living will doesn't take effect even if we are only occasionally of clear mind. Most of us, especially when we are elderly, move back and forth from clear to unclear mind because of the effects of disease, medication, anesthesia, terror, or aging. If we have rational moments, we will be asked to make decisions when we may not know the implications of the decision.

Many people understand, in the lawyer's office or in serious but abstract conversation with family, the meaning of the command "Do Not Resuscitate," but at the unfamiliar and terrifying moment when death is close, someone will call 911 and the ambulance attendants do what they have to do: they restore life.

The best, hardest, and loneliest decision may be not to call the nurse to the hospital bedside or, at home, not to dial 911 but to wait, to talk, to touch, to allow the ultimate gift of death. After caring for Barbara, we hope that each of us or our children will love us enough—and be tough enough—to do what has to be done—or not done.

The nurses who became Barbara's friends helped her go through three surgical procedures in a few days and deal with the tough realities: a permanent catheter and cancer that needed immediate treatment.

She chose to fight, in part I think, because of the care she unexpectedly needed. She would not be alone, but she would be transferred to the Dover Rehabilitation and Living Center that all three of us knew as a nursing home. She faced a long series of radiation treatments, and Art was not at home to care for her.

At first visit, Dover Rehab was as bad as we expected. We saw only the dying and the near dying, those with vacant stares, those who talked to the long dead, those who stared at the blank wall and beyond. The tubes. The wheelchairs. The walkers.

Barbara had been as terrified of nursing homes as we were. It was a common thread in our conversations before she was hospitalized. Consequently, Barbara was disoriented and depressed when she was first transferred to the nursing home, and so were we. We saw what people of our age fear—gap-mouthed old men and women strapped in wheelchairs, some who reached out to touch us, some who spoke sounds that were not language, one who thought we were laughing at her—but we saw the nurses, aides, and technicians treat every patient with respect, concern, and good humor, no matter how difficult they were.

Barbara appreciated their care. She seemed relieved, if not happy to be in a nursing home. Each day we kept popping in early and late, and we began to appreciate the continuous nursing care that was both expert and patient. I often remembered how inexpert our care of Grandmother was at home and how hard it was to be patient caring for her after she lost all sense of time.

At Dover Rehab, Barbara was not treated as another old lady, but the individual of great wit and grand courage we knew. One morning we came in and she told us with delight how the male nurse had bathed and dressed her. "It's been a long time since young male hands have touched this old body."

We were horrified that her first roommate was clearly dying, but Barbara saw that she was needed and could help her. She was not depressed but energized by

being needed. She made friends with another roommate who went home early, she got her hair done, she
learned the ups and downs of the staff's love life.

When Barbara was in the hospital we had been ap-
palled how quickly this very young eighty-five-year-old
aged, but in the dreaded nursing home we saw her
grow young again. Barbara would not have chosen this
adventure, but she knew she was where she needed to
be, and as her daily comrades we became comfortable
visiting in the nursing home, familiar with staff and patients. In the no-longer-dreaded nursing home she was
never alone in the dark and always had someone check-
ing on her who managed to be both professional and
loving.

As in the case of all prejudices, our fear of the nursing home was easier at a distance. These three old
turkeys, Barbara, Minnie Mae, and Don, would just as
soon avoid nursing homes, thank you, but we now
know the quality of human care that is available. I no
longer have the terror of the nursing home that I inherited from my grandmother so very many years ago.

Minnie Mae and I, however, did not at first realize
the full emotional impact of our daily visits with Barbara. Each visit reminded us of where we might end
up. Visiting her in the hospital and nursing home, doing rather intimate errands for her—getting the kind of
dental adhesive she liked, finding a pair of slippers that
would not skid—made both of us aware not only of

what might happen but of what was already happening. I was caring for Barbara as I was becoming a caretaker for Minnie Mae.

The years since sixty have been the best of my life, but that is, in part, because the terrors and shadows of aging make the commonplace exceptional, the ordinary worth celebration. Still, dragons lie in ambush and I confronted them every time I visited Barbara. Over sixty, the fears that were once imagined become real. We confront illness and loss with increasing frequency and there is no place to hide. The dragons attack and we must confront them with shield and sword.

Once in a while, in the hospital or nursing home, Barbara talked of death, of seeing Art again, or of being so lonely she was ready to go. And meeting death as it lurked just outside her door—or in the next bed behind the drawn curtain—Minnie Mae and I found we had to develop our own strengths—and we did. Minnie Mae, observing Barbara's decisions about cancer, did not know she would have to make her own cancer decisions in a few months and that Barbara's radiation doctor would be her own. In the comradeship of war I discovered that it was easier to deal with the known as horrible as it might be than to imagine the unknown. Barbara was an instructive comrade, and as so often happens, as we were helping her, we were helping ourselves.

We were with Barbara during her single visit back to

her home, brought there by a van for the handicapped. She seemed distracted, a stranger in her own house, quickly tired and eager to return to the suddenly familiar and comforting world of the nursing home.

We learned a great deal during our comradeship with Barbara. We discovered that as treatments fail and we pass from hospital to nursing home, most of the doctors disappear. We learned to be grateful for the few who do not, but also learned to not stay angry at a system we cannot change. Their disappearance may indeed be a matter of economics or insurance restrictions, but it is just as likely to be a matter of priority. The doctors' job is to heal, and they must give priority to those who can benefit from treatment. Doctors do care for their patients and I can only imagine the emotional price they pay when they lose a patient. But the doctors' primary job is diagnosis and treatment, not long-term care.

We discovered that the profession of caring—nursing—survives. As the doctors disappear, the nurses and the nurse's aides become more and more visible. We both have benefited from the care of nurses in our own hospital experiences, but in caring for Barbara, we observed, with a critical detachment, at least a hundred nurses and nurse's aides at Wentworth-Douglass Hospital and at the Dover Rehabilitation and Living Center as they cared for Barbara and many other patients. Most were women but several were men, and every single one was caring. No exceptions. They knew Barbara as an individual, treated her with respect, answered all our questions with candor, clarity, and concern. They listened to Barbara, responded to her needs, kept her comfortable, gossiped with her, laughed with her, and grew sad with her when that was appropriate.

One night early on when Barbara was delusional and terrified, a young male nurse sat with her for hours holding her hand and talking to her—long after his shift was finished. One day when Barbara refused food and water during her last days at Dover Rehab, a nurse's aide offered a hug and when Barbara, in a suddenly strong voice said, "I'd like that," the aide lay down on top of the covers and held her in her arms for fifteen or twenty minutes.

After Barbara returned to Wentworth-Douglass Hospital for the last time, Diane Erwin, head nurse on her ward at Dover Rehab, after a long day of caring for her own patients, visited Barbara in the hospital and soothed her lips with ice. If we linger on as Barbara did, we hope our children and friends will visit us, of course, but we know now that we will be in the care of nurses, not doctors, and that they will give us the medications and injections we may need, monitor our condition, respond to our needs, feed us and quench our thirst, get us up, keep us clean, turn us, and, all the time, talk to us as individuals, with respect and love, touching us even after we no longer respond.

In a strange and wonderful way, the further Barbara moved away from us, passing painlessly into a final coma, the more intimate we became. Often her gown slipped down or up. Her pride—her white hair "done" every week—became disheveled; her teeth were not in often. She became my Grandmother Smith, whose bed I stood by each morning of my childhood to see if she was still alive; she became Grandmother Murray, whom I was with when she died; my father, mother, daughter, who died when I was not at their side. And above all I felt closer to her, a neighbor and more, not the son she never had, not the husband who had left before, but a close friend who would be there when death stepped into the room.

The last time the hospital called about our neighbor, Barbara Robinson, I expected to be told she had finally passed away. Instead it was an invitation. The end was near. The nurse was offering me the chance to make sure Barbara would not die alone.

I found myself delaying, performing small, unnecessary tasks around my office, but soon I was on the way to the hospital. The nurse took me in to see Barbara, explained how she knew the end was near, and said she had notified the hospital chaplain. I spoke to Barbara, telling her of all the people who were asking about her and telling her to let go, as I had been instructed by caring nurses in the days before. Then I was silent.

She seemed in no pain. Her eyes were not closed

but they were not seeing, at least not seeing anything that I could see. The only sound was her shallow breathing, and I realized that all the tubes and needles and pumps and wires and meters and gauges and machines that had often been her companions in the past ninety-four days had been removed. She had passed beyond technology.

We could have been alone in a cave above Galilee centuries before the birth of Christ. We were sharing the millennia-old human experience of death, the inevitable and natural end of life. Chaplain Ginny Slawnwhite came in, moved immediately to Barbara's side, took her hand, talked with her, said a prayer, and we both noted that at the word *God* there seemed to be some recognition. She kissed Barbara's forehead.

Before she left, Chaplain Slawnwhite told me she had a community of people whom she had trained to sit with the dying. One such person would relieve me. Barbara had been expected to pass away Monday and it was Friday. I could take a break, have lunch with my grandchildren who were visiting, and return.

When the chaplain left, there was no sadness, no suffering in the room, instead an unexpected peace and companionship. I chatted with Barbara as I had since we moved in across the street thirty-five years ago, read a mystery, and, from time to time, as is my habit, I opened my daybook and wrote. Barbara would understand.

Then the nurse brought Sheila Belsover into the room. I had been told that she had lost a daughter two years ago and that this was one way she was returning the comfort she and her daughter had received. I told her that we, too, had lost a daughter.

I didn't mention that she—and my father and my mother—had died without a family member at their side, attached to machines. I watched with wonder and tears in my eyes as Sheila pulled the chair close to the bed, took Barbara's hand without hesitation, and talked with her. She would not die alone.

I went to lunch with my family, and when I returned, Barbara's door was shut. Dr. Cynthia Cooper, the neighbor who had taken Barbara to the hospital after her fall three months earlier, dropped by for a lunchtime visit, and Sheila, still holding Barbara's hand, said, "I think she has gone." Dr. Cooper certified her death.

Barbara had not died alone. The next time I have an invitation to sit with the dying, I will go quickly, without fear. But next time, I will, as Sheila did, hold the hand of the dying, knowing that touch is the most profound and the final human communication.

My comradeship with the aging is not finished. I am comrade to Minnie Mae, to friends, to strangers I will meet along the road, and to myself. On many mornings I come downstairs and am swept into a fast-running current of images, sounds, smells, feelings—all of the life I have lived, am living, may live—that carries me toward where I do not know. I live again my morning chore of seeing if my grandmother made it through the night, all the deaths in my war, Grandma Smith's dying, which I did not attend, Grandma Murray's, which I did, the deaths of my father, mother, daughter, the suicides when I had to be with the survivors, my mother-in-law, my brother-in-law, my friend's husband, George, Art, Dwight, all my own dyings—imagined and real— during a sickly childhood, in combat, in old age, and now Barbara. And somehow, because of Barbara's gift of comradeship, her allowing us to witness her life and her death, I am more familiar with death and less fearful of what is, for all of us, inevitable.

Chapter 19

LETTING GO

L etting go hasn't been as easy as I expected. I have
reflected upon the past, giving each moment a special texture through this twice-lived life, but I have
lived not in the past but in the moment illuminated by
the past. I have made powerful, personal commitments
to the task at hand, volunteering for the paratroops,
seeking to do fast-breaking news stories on deadline,
preferring to teach beginning students rather than
those who can teach themselves. Feeling humble, shy,
inadequate, I have always wanted to be in charge.

Still, I have not been one for returning, attending
reunions, trying to live a life that is no longer mine.
I can't remember feeling nostalgia, found it easy to
leave school, the army, newspapers, and magazines
on my own volition or theirs, to move to a new neighborhood. I have even found it easy, to my surprise, to
turn over the direction of programs I initiated and developed at the university to others, no second-guessing,
no regrets. It was easy to retire from the university

197

thirteen years ago, and I have never once wanted to return.

I never joined the youth religion of so many Americans. I came home from my war with a streak of white hair and was happy to see it grow and extend. No hair dye for me. Wear bifocals, trifocals? Okay. A hearing aid? I'll wear one, and if the big kind on the outside of the ear is more efficient, let me have it. I have, of course, dieted but it really didn't worry me when I turned from a string bean into an eggplant. The letting go of aging would be easy.

And yet . . .

In my early seventies Minnie Mae would find me sitting forward in my morris chair, studying my shoes as if I had just discovered I had feet.

"What's wrong?" she'd ask.

"Nothing," I'd answer—of course.

But there was something wrong. It was too silly to mention. The winterized porch on which we spend most of our time has windows running along each of three sides, and the room is bright with sun and light even on dreary New England days. At night, since we are readers and have multibulb reading lamps that fill the room with light, I still felt the room growing dark, the walls of windows moving closer and closer, the ceiling lowering. There was a strange coldness in my belly I had never felt before, even alone in a foxhole under shellfire, and a greater feeling of despair than I had felt during the terrible days of my daughter's dying.

When Minnie Mae spoke to me, I always found myself in the same position, elbows on knees, bent over, examining my shoes, the way the laces were tied or, if I was barefoot, the pattern of my long bony toes.

It didn't happen every night—or even every other night—but when the darkness came on, it was usually just before suppertime when I had had a glass of wine or two—to prevent my second heart attack, of course—or when I took my second of three pill feedings. I would force myself to eat—a new experience—lifting each forkful as if it weighed a hundred pounds, the fastest gulper in the East slowly chewing, slowly swallowing, concentrating on each bite, promising myself I had to eat only just this one. And then, when it was swallowed, forcing myself to take in just one more forkful. And then another. And another. It was a dull, tedious process to perform, and it must have been agonizing for Minnie Mae to watch.

It was spooky. More often than not, exactly thirty-nine minutes after the meal was finished, the room would grow bright, the walls of windows draw back, the ceiling rise, the coldness in my gut disappear. If the despair hit at other times and I could write, the darkness would rise during the writing.

I had always thought I felt sympathetic to those who

suffered depression, but secretly believed they could snap out of it. I'd given up a four-pack-a-day cigarette habit overnight and stopped drinking for twenty-four years. I told myself to snap out of it, but I didn't snap.

I remembered that alcohol was a depressant. I skipped the wine. No change. I tried the wine. No change.

It must be the pills. I called the doctor and we changed prescriptions and the hours the pills were taken. No difference. The darkness returned. Not every night, but enough to frighten me.

I had always been scornful of those in my family and those with whom I worked or supervised who did not go into counseling, and I praised those who did, but I found myself with the Scots, Yankee, male reluctance to seek help common to my generation. Finally I gave in and asked the doctor for the name of a psychiatrist. If I had a broken leg, I'd go to the doctor; if I had a broken spirit, I'd better get to a psychiatrist.

I went to the one he recommended. The psychiatrist was round-and-beaming faced, as natty as a Kentucky undertaker, and I didn't really want to talk to him, but I talked about my born-again childhood, my war, the loss of our daughter, the stuff I thought from seeing movies that a psychiatrist would want to hear. Hardly listening to me he prescribed alprazolam.

"Take half a pill. If that doesn't work, take another half. Then another half or more. If you find yourself sitting there with a stupid smile on your face, you've taken enough." His diagnosis of panic attacks was wrong but the treatment okay. Then he talked of *his* born-again Catholicism, what it meant to *him*, and asked how I could not believe and survive. He seemed astonished at my mental health, unsure of his own, and even appeared to envy my escape from religion. He did not show me his penis tree that, according to later newspaper reports, he showed to some women patients.

I left confused, confirmed in my fear that to be a crazy doctor you had to be crazy, but filled the prescription. A few nights later, the porch grew dark, the ceiling lowered, and my shoes became incredibly fascinating. Minnie Mae reminded me of my funny pills, and without any faith that anything would or could help, I broke the tiny pill and swallowed the speck of medication. Half a pill worked. In ninety seconds the ceiling rose, the room grew bright, my shoes seemed just my shoes. I rarely reach for that particular drug these days, but there is one in my pocket right now as I write, just in case. I took one last night in fact.

When the prescription ran out, I went back to my doctor-dealer. He had told me that to get this pill refilled, I had to get a new prescription. That turned out not to be true. Without asking me about how the pill worked, he scrawled out a new prescription and then again asked me how I lived without faith, especially after the death of my daughter. He kept probing my feelings as if I knew what he needed to know, leaning forward to listen intently to me. I felt I had been cast in some Woody Allen movie in which the patient becomes psychiatrist. I fled.

I called a friend who had a psychiatrist in the family, who saw a therapist himself, and whose judgment I respected. He referred me to a different practice and I found Dr. Mary Wilson, a young woman who listened. In the whirlpool of her attentive listening, I was carried back through all my professional life, past the death of my daughter, past my months in combat, back to the cliché of my unhappy childhood and its effect on my life today.

I no longer go every week. At the moment I am seeing her every other week, but soon I will take another vacation from therapy. I usually feel a bit foolish and self-indulgent as I drive to an appointment and sit quietly observing the strange courtesies of the psychiatric waiting room: do not make eye contact unless the other person does it first; do not stare; do not recognize a friend, colleague, or acquaintance unless they recognize you.

I am always early for my appointment, the doctor always late, and she makes me go ahead of her down the long corridor to her office at the farthest end, where I take the large flowered armchair that is almost a love seat with its back in the window alcove, and she sits across from me and to my right. The office is pleasantly—and neutrally—feminine, the box of tissues I have used only once near my right hand.

We have evolved what I like to call a professional friendship. I know of her life what I know of most of my doctors' lives. She has a husband and two boys. We have shared the hurricane damage to her out-of-state property, the death of her father and, later, her mother, and her recent surgery—all because the events meant canceling appointments. She was a nurse who became a doctor serving in an emergency room before becoming a psychiatrist.

There is no doubt the therapy works. I have few of the severe attacks that sent me into therapy. Every once in a while, for no rational reason—if it was rational, would I go to a psychiatrist?—a river of sadness flows underneath an apparently happy life. I find myself fearing I will die before this book is done; the world seems flat, devoid of taste, color, feeling; my feet are trapped in quicksand. I go back to Dr. Wilson. We talk and she may adjust the medication. I have a far greater understanding of how my past influences my present, and I have modified my behavior, being a better husband, and can now wash my hair without pain.

Silly as it seems, shampooing was the convincer for me. I hated to wash my hair. It hurt. I thought my scalp was peculiarly sensitive, because each time I shampooed I felt my mother's fingers digging into my scalp and felt my skull banging against the faucets in the sink. This was so silly I hardly admitted it to myself and never told anyone, wife or therapist, about it. But one day I washed my hair and no pain. My scalp wasn't sensitive. My mother's fingers no longer dug into my skull. Therapy worked.

I am not sure how. I sit in my chair. She sits in hers. We begin casually as if we were meeting for lunch but soon I am talking. No surprise there, I am a talker, and she listens, no surprise there, that's her trade. Occasionally she will question me, "Can you remember a time when your mother touched you, perhaps just on the shoulder in a loving way when you sat at the kitchen table, or sat down and said she understood something you had said or done?"

That's an easy question, I think, almost a dumb question. Of course I can. But after long thought, not one time. My mother did shake my hand—one pump—when I left for war and again—one pump—when I unexpectedly returned. But no spontaneous touches, no signs of affection or approval. Nothing.

I am not without friends but blessed with many of them. I wonder why I need this professional friendship. Minnie Mae is my best friend, but she does not like to talk about feelings—hers or mine—and I, like some emotional porcupine, have feelers extending in all directions. In this way we reverse the stereotypical roles in marriage. Minnie Mae does not like to con-

sider, examine, study, admit, reveal, share her feelings
or mine. I have friends such as Chip Scanlan and Don
Graves with whom I can and do share feelings, even
the most uncomfortable ones that I share with my therapist. That is good therapy but they are friends and not
professionals. Their reactions are greatly affected by
their caring for me, their evolving experiences with our
shared craft of writing, and the projections that come
from their own biographies. My therapist has a professional perspective.

I had always wondered if I had made up my unhappy
childhood, but it turns out that my childhood was
worse than I admitted. It was strangely helpful to re-
experience it—good and bad—to put it in the perspective of the life I have lived since childhood and
to understand how it has affected me, again for good
and bad.

It turns out that the brief, intense depressions I had
are fairly normal for men in their seventies, and I wish
more men of my generation who need help would get
it. I don't understand how my treatment works. I do
take a minimum dose of an antidepressant but more
helpful, I believe, are the conversations.

Some depression is normal in aging. It is a tough
landscape and gets tougher the longer the trek. I think
there are at least three stages of aging. The first is the
sixties and the early to midseventies, when we are in
relatively good health and often, in our society, rather

well-off financially. I have been younger in habit, activity, attitude, and dress at seventy-five than my father or mother were at fifty-five. In this first stage of aging, we are not really old.

But eventually old age becomes a grim business. Our destination is all too clear. We pass into a middle old age when our health is not quite as good; when we cannot travel with our former ease, if at all; when one of us—in my case Minnie Mae, who had her eighty-first birthday soon after my seventy-sixth—ages faster than the other. We study our partners—and ourselves—for signs of aging and spot them. We lose family, neighbors, and friends to nursing homes and funeral parlors. Some live on but no longer recognize us. We have to pack away the dreams we delayed fulfilling until it was too late, and we have the old hurts that haunt us: what was done and can't be undone; what was not done and can't be done; what was said and can't be unsaid; what was not said and can never be said.

Ahead is, if I am lucky, the final stage of aging—eighty-five? ninety? ninety-five?—when I expect I will say "better than the alternative." The horizons will grow closer, the limitations greater, but despite the grim realities I have known, I have a confidence typical of my generation.

We survived the Great Depression and World War II, recession and upswing, bypasses and the loss of loved ones, and through it all, our unexpected survival has made most of us optimists. Not necessarily about the world—although it seems, for all its faults, a far better place to me than it was when I was young—but quietly, even secretly, confident about our individual ability to cope. As Minnie Mae once said as she faced another CAT scan—or was it another MRI?—"I've been tested and I passed. I don't need another testing."

Recently there has been a tendency to romanticize our generation. "I don't know if I could do what you guys did," says the man who sits in front of us at hockey games, speaking of his father and me. He could. He is a good man and a strong one, but he hasn't been asked to undergo the same historical experiences and so he does not have the assurance that many of us old-timers do that he can take it.

Writing this book I have discovered many things about my life—and the lives of my generation—but the most surprising to me are the opportunities we were given by the times in which we lived and the advantages of adversity.

As a teenager in the Depression, I had the opportunity of grown-up jobs as well as boy's work. I was cheap and no one was paying attention to laws against hiring kids if there were any laws limiting our activities. I could do a man's work—drive a truck, chauffeur a state official, make sausage, reorganize a real estate office, work nights in the advertising department of a newspaper— as long as I showed up on time and did the job well. I had a man's job and a man's standards. I also could get hired as a teenager and I could get fired as a teenager.

I seized control of my life, never realizing what I was doing. I got jobs or quit school and told my parents afterwards. I was learning my own way in the world, making stupid mistakes but learning from them. I knew how to get a job and learned how to do it while doing it. No training programs. If I wanted something—a bike, skates, a car—I had to know how to get it with my own money. I was in charge of my own education, flunking out of high school on my own stupidity, fitting a year of college in before the war and paying for it myself.

The United States Army—and the enemy army— didn't treat me as an adolescent. Eighteen was a man's age with a man's job to do. We faced responsibility for those with whom we trained and fought, and we accepted responsibility for ourselves. After the war many of us seized the opportunity of the G.I. Bill that paid our college tuition, and we explored the territory that had been almost exclusively the province of the well-to-do. My father had not been allowed to go to high school by his father. I went to college on my own. My father was distantly proud and, I am sure, somewhat concerned that college might take me away from his Baptist church and his Republican Party—as it did.

An education and an expanding economy gave us more control over our lives than our parents ever had. I could choose a career—great poet who wrote an occasionally fine novel—and I did. Of course, that career track didn't provide food and there was no family money, only family debts, so I became a newspaperman, the generic term of the times. I would work with language for the rest of my life; I made money doing what I wanted to do. Well, not exactly what I wanted to do. The great poems and fine novels are yet to come, but I put dinner on the table without heavy lifting. I wrote news stories and editorials and columns and magazine articles and corporate annual reports and academic articles and textbooks and some novels, short stories, and poems. I had a great deal of control over my life, and even when I was fired by *Time* magazine, I survived in New York City freelancing for other national magazines and working on a few books. Most of the time I chose what I would write and when and how. It didn't always get published but we always ate, and later I even survived the shark-infested waters of campus politics.

The name of my game was control. I liked being in charge of my life. I am the one who likes to initiate the plans, make the reservations, drive the car. I like to be in charge, and retirement, at first, increases the opportunity for control. No meetings. No bosses. Nobody to supervise. No schedule but your own. No writing assignments you do not want. Time to travel where you want to travel—the Alaskan and Scandinavian north, Holland and Canada, Switzerland and Greece, Scotland, Tuscany.

Now the trips overseas are out. Not the flight but the airports and the standing in line have become too difficult for Minnie Mae. Bedtime comes earlier—after the evening nap. There is energy, but it is rationed. There is still control, but there are constraints, considerations, limitations.

I found myself refusing to read the Sunday travel sections. It was hard to give up the return to Tuscany and the Hebrides, harder to realize the Antarctic, New Zealand, Japan would never be seen. Driving at night is still possible but less pleasant. The quick trip to Boston to a museum or a game became a question, then out of the question.

Minnie Mae seems better at letting go than I am. Perhaps she is wiser or has fewer dreams, is a realist or has less need for control. We reassess our myths about ourselves and each other. I realize that she was not quite as independent as she seemed—or as she spoke. She takes to a certain dependence with grace. Our tensions have a new cast. Minnie Mae's response to an invitation, a proposal, a vacation, a trip has always been negative. I have had to overcome the inertia. "We can't afford it" can be argued against but not her back, her weariness, the diabetes, the Parkinson's. I have to push but cannot, in fairness, push too hard.

Hardest of all, for her, was giving up the garden. It is not something we can do together. She loves to garden. I hate working in the yard. She wants things done her way. Her way is obvious—to her, not to me. I hate taking orders and know I will screw up—and, of course, I do.

We have help once a week to clean and now someone to do the accounts. We had, in the beginning of our marriage, decided it was healthy to air the beds during the day. It is not hard for us to give up a level of housecleaning we had never attempted anyway. Minnie Mae cooks less. It is her territory and I am not to enter despite the fact that I cooked in our earlier years. We eat out more and more. Doesn't bother me but it makes Minnie Mae feel guilty.

And I have to admit my own limitations. I can lift weights, but I can't prove my manliness by lifting other things. I have to ask for help, even asking our daughters to do the heavy lifting.

I suggest moving the washer and drier from the basement to the second floor. Minnie Mae refuses to consider it. We have plans to move the bedroom down to the first floor, my office and the laundry up to the first floor, but so far Minnie Mae won't discuss implementing the plans.

We are clear that we do not want to move into a retirement community where assisted living is available or to live near or with our children. It is the issue of control more than anything else. I fear the control of the community. I would be expected to wear socks all year long and cover my suspenders in the dining room; our daughters would control our schedules and our habits. We fear loss of control above all else. And yet we realize those decisions may be taken away from us as we lose control.

This later stage of aging is not all bad. I remember my shock when I marched to my first battle and saw the piles of gas masks, bedrolls, all the nonessentials that were heaped by the road from those who went before. And I remember the freedom of my own stripping down.

We are less burdened by obligations and appearances, becoming more ourselves, fighting to preserve what is most important to us as the horizons grow closer. I treasure the twice-lived life, the old stories told and retold as the meanings I need to hear come clear. I live then and now.

My job now may be to help Minnie Mae out of bed and to fasten the bra—the ironic reversal of what was once my intent—but the passion survives, to my surprise, and the world is made rich with the quiet companionship we treasure more and more, the shared laugh, the gesture, the glance, the touch, the lives that have been interwoven into one.

We have family, old friends and new, and we have newspapers, magazines, and books to read. We read in the car, in the waiting room, and in our reading chairs, entering the pages as we did when we first discovered the magic of reading so many years ago. If our eyes hold out, there will always be books to read, and if not, books to hear.

I will continue to write and to draw. I will see the world through word and line. One December morning I sat on the porch taking pleasure in a winter fog. I drew, in my mind, the gray winter trees against the gray of the fog, delighting in the two, three, a dozen, more shades of gray, the palette ranging from black to white and all the grays in between. Once this book is done, I will paint that and if I don't, I have painted it in my mind and it hangs in the museum of my skull, waiting to be examined again.

Looking into my foggy woods, I tell myself stories of a London fog and a death when I was on military police duty in Piccadilly Circus, of waking as a boy on a mountaintop in New Hampshire and seeing a single church steeple rise through the clouds below, of a snow fog in the Battle of the Bulge and the ghost battalions of Germans advancing, of the rolling cliff of ocean fog that raced toward Uncle Don's Friendship Sloop before my war. I listen from my chair and hear—so clear—the low moan of a foghorn that sounded off the coast of Nantucket in 1940 and still haunts my ear. I feel the fog damp my skin, smell the fog in my wool shirt, know that if I sit here quietly, waiting, I will see a dark shape in the fog. It will come closer, become a man or woman, and if I am patient, the person will tell me his or her story. There always is a story. I may write it but even if I can no longer hold a pen, type, or even dictate, I will always have narrative as my companion. Of story there will be no letting go.